A YEAR
IN PLACE

A YEAR
IN PLACE

EDITED BY

W. Scott Olsen

Bret Lott

THE UNIVERSITY OF UTAH PRESS
Salt Lake City

© 2001 by the University of Utah Press

Printed on acid-free paper

ISBN 0-87480-673-9

LIBRARY OF CONGRESS CATALOGING-IN-PUBLICATION DATA

A year in place / edited by W. Scott Olsen and Bret Lott.
   p.   cm.
  ISBN 0-87480-673-9 (alk. paper)
   1. Authors, American—20th century—Homes and haunts. 2. Authors,
American—20th century—Biography. 3. Authorship. 4. Months.
I. Olsen, W. Scott, 1958–   II. Lott, Bret. III. Title.
  PS135 Y43 2000
  810.9'0054—dc21   00-011011

06   05   04   03   02   01   00
5   4   3   2   1

CONTENTS

A YEAR IN PLACE: AN INTRODUCTION

BRET LOTT

For what else is there, but time and place?
What more, but chronos and geos?

ONE

HERE IS A STORY, ONE I HAVEN'T WRITTEN DOWN BEFORE, BUT that I've told a hundred times.

We'd been here in Charleston for four or five years by then — we've been here for fourteen — and as often happens no matter what job you have, it seemed the grass was greener somewhere else. I hadn't taken to the college's Department of English as quickly or as well as I had hoped. I was here to write and to teach, but the former just didn't seem to be getting enough attention.

And there was the fact I and my family had moved here to the Deep South. I was born and raised in southern California, with a pocket of years in the middle of my childhood spent in Phoenix, Arizona. In moving here, I discovered the truth of what most everyone had warned me about: even after living here for four or five years, there were still certain cultural elements to which I hadn't yet become acclimated. Chief among them the fact of how slow time plays out down here.

The notion of fast food, for example, is a textbook illustration of the term "oxymoron." And people here, when driving residential streets, are prone to slowing to a stop and hanging out their car windows to converse with acquaintances on the front porches of homes. A pleasant thing to do, I have to admit, but if you are in the car behind the one whose driver is conversing with those on a porch, and if you learned to drive on the freeways of Los Angeles, there can be no more annoying and frustrating and condescending directive than the driver, once he's noticed you in the rearview mirror, raising high his hand and waving you around in what must seem to him a magnanimous signal of patience and kindness.

I wasn't too happy here.

On this particular autumn afternoon so many years ago—an afternoon, despite the passage of time, still clear and certain and true in its detail and spirit—I'd dropped off Zeb, who must have been seven or eight, at his karate studio, a storefront shop where the floors were lined with mats, and seven- and eight-year-old kids all in rows practiced their blocks, katas, and pinyans. The class was led by Mr. Mike, a young master from south Boston, his thick street accent a wonderful and refreshing reminder among the sweet drawl everywhere around us of when we lived in Massachusetts, where I went to grad school and where Zeb was born.

We lived in a duplex then, the yard out front no real yard at all but an asphalt parking strip accented here and there with redtips and crepe myrtle. Melanie must have been working late at the architectural firm she was a secretary for downtown, because I'd had to round up both Zeb and his younger brother, Jake, alone from where they rode their bikes out on the asphalt, then make sure Zeb got dressed in his white *ghi,* then get them both into the van and headed for karate.

But at the last moment, both boys finally strapped in, me coming around the front of the van and headed for my door, I stopped, saw Jake's kiddie bike there on the sidewalk newly shorn of its training wheels—he was four or five, and proud of the accomplishment finding his balance had been—and for no good reason other than that I thought it might be fun, I picked up the bike and put it into the back of the van, Jake and Zeb both twisting in their seats to see what the big idea was.

"We're going over to Alhambra Hall while you work out," I said to Zeb. "Jake needs to practice riding his bike," I said, and pulled closed the back door.

The two of them faced forward, Jacob smiling at Zeb, I could see in the rearview mirror once I'd climbed in, with the kind of antagonistically cavalier smile only siblings can muster one for the other. Jacob and I'd sat together through any number of sessions at the studio, the two of us on the wooden bench at the rear of the room, watching all the moves and listening to the proper shouts at the appointed times enough to where I knew the whole thing was a bore for Jacob. He was a soccer player, and this inside stuff just wasn't for him. Hence, this smile. He and Dad were going to go do something different.

Zeb, of course, ignored Jacob.

We left the studio, drove down McCants toward Alhambra Hall, the street shrouded in live oak dripping Spanish moss. This was the Old Village, the original part of town where the homes themselves were just as shrouded as the street. We passed the old cemetery on the right, where a couple of times a year church groups and Boy Scouts and sometimes families in town banded together and cleaned things up, the tombstones in there going all the way back to the Revolution, all of them, too, shrouded in those trees.

Up ahead I could see where McCants ended, the break in the trees at the street's dead end where the marsh began, and the harbor lay.

Then we were at that dead end, and here to my left stood Alhambra Hall, the old two-story building on a parcel of land overlooking Charleston Harbor the town owned and rented out for weddings and for Jazzercise, and where the crafts festival was held twice a year, the town's Halloween Haunted House as well. And this was where each year the Blessing of the Fleet is celebrated, most everyone in town turning out for the fried shrimp and funnel cakes, the face paintings and shrimp-shelling contest, and then the big moment when the bishop stands down by the water and blesses the shrimping fleet, each trawler slowly cruising past out on the harbor in a hometown parade of boats.

But this afternoon there was no one at the place, the acre or so of land Alhambra Hall stood on empty, the sloping lawn behind it that fell gently down to the marsh ready for us two.

I nosed the van into the parking spot in front of the hall, Jake already unbuckled and reaching for the door. I went around back, opened the van door, and pulled out the bike, and could only watch as Jacob, smiling not at me but at that bike as though it were some steed only he had been able to finesse into a means of transportation, climbed on and took off. I wasn't involved here. This was about him, and about his bike.

He broke then for the grass out back of the hall, and I had no choice but to trail behind him on the concrete sidewalk and around the building and out onto the lawn, before us both now the wide spread of grass, beyond it the marsh, the yellow grass and marsh grass and salt hay that made up the all of it. And beyond that lay the water itself, the mile or so–wide stretch of glass reflecting the sun low on the horizon, that horizon the church spires and old homes of Charleston itself.

It was beautiful.

Scattered here and there across the lawn were park benches, wrought iron and wood slatted and placed here, I knew, for just such moments as these. I went to the one closest, sat down, Jacob now riding his bike off toward the marsh edge, then turning, heading back toward me, still smiling, though still with his eyes not to me, but to the ground, to the handlebars, to the wheel out in front of him, and to the handlebars again.

Now he was doing figure eights a few feet in front of me, his eyebrows furrowed in concentration, the smallest tip of his tongue poking out the side of his mouth the way he will do. He was doing figure eights, performing a kind of magic perhaps he'd only dreamed himself capable of doing before last week, when we'd finally taken off those training wheels.

This was autumn, the air starting to cool down enough to allow for this sort of late-afternoon excursion, the biting gnats not out yet for the fact it was still too warm, and not yet quite cool enough.

And this was autumn, when the first of the job listings arrived in the mail, like some sort of siren song of life being better elsewhere, of lighter teaching loads, of colleagues who were more predictable and congenial and less likely to pop at any moment. I'd seen in the first salvo of opportunities that'd arrived the week before a few places that looked interesting.

This was autumn. There would be decisions to make. There would be bridges to cross.

And still Jacob made figure eights in front of me, his whole life, I saw, given over in this moment to the concentrated effort and fulfilling payoff of steering that handlebar the way it needed to go.

That was when I looked up from him, and from the grass, and from my life spent thinking grass somewhere else just had to be greener, to see cutting across the reflection of the setting sun on the harbor a shrimp trawler headed for home, its hull pure white and sharp on the water, its seine nets hauled in and high on either side of the boat, like hands held together in prayer.

And then, as though this weren't gift enough to me, as though this weren't as blunt and bludgeoning a sign of the beauty of this time and place, and hence reason enough to stay here and never leave, there came next three or four dolphins arcing in the trawler's wake, following the shrimp boat home as if this were a game of chase.

Dolphins, arcing, their backs glistening in that setting sun, I could see, in the brief moments they were out of the water.

All this: a setting sun on water, the marsh, the boat, those dolphins. And my son, doing figure eights.

"Look!" I said to Jacob then. "Look at the dolphins out there!"

He stopped, still with that tip of the tongue poking out, and quick put a foot to the ground, turned toward the water. He squinted for the light down on us, and smiled.

I've told that story a hundred times. It's my answer to why I live where I do, an answer inherently tied to the fact of time and place and the intractable hold the precise moment they are married one to the other can have on the human heart.

But sometimes I wonder.

Would I still be living where I do, for instance, if the temperature had been a degree or two off, and I'd been swatting at those damned biting gnats that infest this place for a few weeks each spring and fall? Would we still be here if Jake had fallen and, say, broken his chin on the concrete sidewalk that surrounds Alhambra Hall?

Would we still be here if I hadn't tossed that kiddie bike into the back of the van, or if we'd simply stayed at the studio and watched, bored, while Zeb went through yet again another set of blocks?

And have things remained as idyllic as they were that afternoon so long ago, so that the choice to stay has proved to be the correct one, though made in the smallest of moments?

Does it matter that Jazzercise is no longer held at the hall, but now meets at the new rec center, named after the mayor who saw this town through the cataclysm of Hurricane Hugo and its aftermath? Does it matter that the town has grown so big that the Haunted House is now held at the high school gym, and that the crafts festival shows up at the National Guard Armory now for how big it has grown too?

Does it make a difference that Zeb gave up karate years ago, stands six-foot-two and wears a size-fifteen shoe, and that Jacob is taller than his mom, worries over which brand of deodorant he should use, and rides his bike only for the utility it affords in getting him to his best friend Matt's house, the aesthetic quality of a figure eight only a dim memory at best?

And is the galvanizing memory of a precise moment in time on a precise point on planet Earth made brittle enough to break by the fact that on an afternoon a little more than a year after that evening sun and those figure eights, our mayor, the same one for whom the rec center is named, pulled up to Alhambra Hall, told the groundskeeper to come get him from that bench over there in about half an hour in case he fell asleep, and then walked across the lawn, seated himself at the bench—the same one I sat on a year earlier to watch my reason for staying here unfold—and put a gun to his head, and pulled the trigger, so distraught he was at some business dealings gone bad?

Of course, asking these sorts of questions is pointless.

What matters is that we have stayed.

Time passes, places change, as do people. None of which alters that afternoon, that moment when time and place began to prevail over the history only I owned up to that moment, and the history only I would accrue from that point forward.

But I've never written down that moment, never stopped to ponder over which written words might capture as precisely and truly as can be what it was I remember happening that afternoon.

And what I have found in writing these words down, in recording my own moment of time and place—is that chronos and geos can be offered up only to those who were not present, and in that offering be found to have meaning.

The word. That's what gives significance to what we have witnessed in our lives, what makes chronos and geos transcend themselves to become, in the miraculous alchemy of language attended and informed and guided by the heart and soul, understanding.

Which is what we hope this book will bring you: an understanding—recorded in the disparate and kindred spirit languages of the poem and story, the essay and journal—of the human condition, revealed, as it can only and always be revealed, in the scant and fleeting days afforded us, and in the places we find ourselves blessed enough to be.

W. SCOTT OLSEN

T W O

Somewhere, the storm is assembling itself. Cold air from the Beaufort Sea is beginning to sink and spin. High pressure. Clear sky moves ashore at Tuktoyaktuk in the Canadian Northwest Territories, and, pushed by a familiar winter bend in the jet stream, it follows the Mackenzie River south. Past the Great Bear Lake. Past Yellowknife. Past Edmonton and then Medicine Hat. Finally, it reaches eastern Montana or western North Dakota.

This cold air, however, is not enough by itself. From the west a small low-pressure cell, a weak cold front, arrives. This adds energy, and water. Gathered from the Pacific Ocean, from the Yellowstone and Missouri Rivers, from farm ponds and birdbaths and grocery store parking lots, this water smells like snow.

Cold, wet, heavy air tumbling out of the Bitterroot or Absaroka Range, moving into the open lands of eastern Montana or western North Dakota. And the colder air from north of Alaska. The western air rides up over the northern air, and the water condenses to snow. This is enough for winter. But it's still not enough for the storm.

It always happens, though. Sometimes only once or twice in a year. Sometimes five or six or seven times in a row. An atmospheric trough forms, and water from the Gulf of Mexico, lots of water, suddenly races northward, up the eastern slopes of the Rocky Mountains, past Houston or Corpus Christi on its way to Lubbock, Colorado Springs,

Denver, Laramie, Casper, Sheridan. On television, some weather-person will unfailingly call this The Moisture Express. This water is too much for the waiting cold air, so it turns to snow. Yet the water keeps coming. It keeps turning to snow. The energy builds.

As the rotation of the earth moves the storm eastward, men and women at the National Weather Service in Grand Forks, North Dakota, watch their radars and pressure maps. Winter Storm Watch, they say. Winter Weather Advisory. Winter Storm Warning. Blizzard Warning.

In December, in western Minnesota, every day begins with the weather. How cold? How long until the storm? It's often colder here than it is at the North Pole, and the windchill can pass eighty degrees below zero. We've all heard the stories about the lost, and the frozen, and the dead.

This particular December, however, the ground is still bare. There was a rumor of some flurries a few days ago, ten or fifteen seconds of light sleet, but then nothing. Because we know this place, because we have a history here, the open ground and warm air are more troubling than not.

We all know the blizzard is coming. It's just late. In this place, in this month, the weather will turn hard.

December, in Minnesota, is a cold month. At Halloween, the weather has already begun to turn, and children wear winter coats under their monster suits. By Thanksgiving, we're normally one or two good snows into the season. When the calendar changes to the last month, we're not surprised at all when the forecast says cold. The men and women on television and radio use that word every night. Cold tonight. Cold tomorrow. A little colder tomorrow night. A little less cold the day after that. Then continued cold. Cold for now. Cold for later.

In the early morning, we have a routine. My daughter's school bus comes to collect her for fourth grade at 7:03 A.M. At 6:15, I walk into her room and gather her up, carry her downstairs, and deposit her on the living room couch while I make her a bowl of cereal, either hot or cold, or perhaps toast. When the food is ready, she gets up, eats, and then goes upstairs again to get dressed. At 6:45, the real work begins. Her blue coat goes on. The zipper is zipped and the

Velcro flap secured. The gloves go on. The superinsulated boots. The mad-bomber hat gets pulled down over her head and snapped under her chin.

Because this morning isn't really *that* cold, somewhere around ten below zero, we've left her insulated snow pants in her backpack with her books.

The driveway has become a sheet of ice by this time in the winter, as have the street and curve where we live. When we see the bus coming, my wife and I open our front door, kiss our daughter farewell, and watch her shuffle-step on the ice. She stops about halfway down, knowing the bus may slide a bit on the street ice, then continues when the bus doors open to her. All the way, my wife and I watch the small white clouds of breath that mist and twirl around her hat.

"Cold," I say to Maureen.

"No kidding," she says.

Our son, in kindergarten, rides to school in the car.

In the distance, I can hear the scraping. Steel on pavement. A City of Moorhead snowplow around a corner someplace, working. One large blade in front, a black rubber damper hung on its top so the snow curls as it's moved like some wave in a surfer's dream. And a retractable side blade for clearing the road's shoulder.

Blizzard warning. Schools closed. Kids at home, their snow pants and boots hung on pegs and shelves back at school.

New snow. Fat. Heavy. Falling this day with lightning, and thunder. On the telephone, a friend of mine says she thinks the world is ending—this lightning in snowfall stuff. I tell her no, it's not ending. Just showing off a bit. This is December, in Minnesota.

But still I stand at the windows of our house, watching this storm, and I am nothing if not filled with wonder. This new snow covers the snow from last week. That snow covered the dusting from the week before. The dusting covered the brown grass. When the wind deepens it sometimes digs, and the older, grayer snow gets lifted and blown and then dropped again. The old snow covering the new. My snowshoes and boots have made holes in the old snow that the new snow covers, and fills. The city plow and my own snowblower churn old snow into new powder and eject it over the yard. The layers are far from even.

So perhaps it's not odd that while watching a December blizzard what I am really thinking about is geology. Layers of rock. Deeper forces then moving that rock. Syncline. Antisyncline. Sometimes the heat and fluid below the layers erupt, and then there's a new story on top, an overburden, or, in between, an intrusion. Sometimes a glacial coldness sweeps over, scraping and piling and rearranging the materials.

It's a perfect metaphor for human living.

Geology is the study of place, of the physical earth, over time. Paleontology, sedimentology, geomorphology, stratigraphy, geophysics, geodesy, geochemistry, mineralogy, crystallography, petrology, structural geology, mining geology, petroleum geology, astrogeology — each is really after the same thing. A partial answer to a simple question.

What is this place, over time?

Of course, the partial answers lead to larger questions. How has this place come to be this place? What forces have been at work here? How can I connect what I see with my eyes, touch with my hands, or read on a gravity map with the other parts of the developing story? The questions are as much for literature as for physical science.

Like literature, geology is an incomplete and thrilling pursuit. Earthquakes. Dinosaurs. Volcanoes. Continents pulling apart or smashing together, making oceans or the Himalayas. And there are stories in the words, in what our spirits hear when they're spoken. Precambrian, Paleozoic, Mesozoic, Cenozoic. Or better yet, Cambrian, Ordovician, Silurian, Devonian, Mississippian, Pennsylvanian, Permian, Triassic, Jurassic, Cretaceous, Tertiary, Quaternary. Or even Pleistocene, Holocene. Each of these names fills our heads with not only how long ago, but also what happened. Pleistocene means where I live was under water, in an arm of a tremendous inland sea called Lake Agassiz. Cretaceous means a Tyrannosaurus Rex stood in my driveway.

Standing at the windows here, I know about geologic time. But what about time geology? If we dug into a month, or into twelve months, what patterns would we see? What folds? What intrusions? What minerals or gems? What layers? What unconformities? What erratics?

A Year in Place is a book about place, over time. Divided into twelve parts, to match the calendar months, in each of these month-chapters we invited these writers to consider that month in their place—whatever that place might be or mean. One writer's place may be a natural setting, and his or her chapter would be very close to what we call natural history. Another writer's place may be social, or historical, or whatever. Poetry. Fiction. Essays. Each of them a way to tell the particular way a place comes to mean something more intimate than the body; each of them a way to describe the shape of a spirit in place. Twelve first-rate writers, each examining a specific time and their environment and concerns—a book that gives voice to the many creative and problematic ways we experience our places in the world.

Time is a way of seeing place, of learning how the stories collect themselves. December, in Minnesota, for example, is a hard, cold, thrilling, and beautiful story. It holds blizzards and sun dogs, lethal cold as well as Advent, and Christmas, and New Year's Eve. December, though, is just one layer. It rests on the November stories, and will be covered by the stories of January. Old Decembers erupt into this one as memories, as do old Julys and Augusts. No layer in time, and no layer in the earth, is pristine.

In every way that matters, place means story. Because stories are how we come to know each other—person to person, person to place, place to history—the intrusions and fault lines and unconformities become acts of illumination. To study them, to open them up for a more public examination, is an act of invitation and love.

Welcome.

EARTHQUAKE
WEATHER

DOROTHY BARRESI

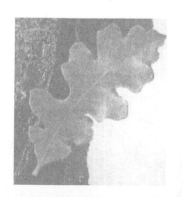

Surface waves in earthquakes can be divided into two
types. The first is called a Love wave.... It moves the
ground from side to side in a horizontal plane but at
right angles to the direction of propagation. The
horizontal shaking of Love waves is particularly
damaging to the foundation of structures.
—Bruce Bolt, *Earthquakes*

THIS STORY BEGINS BETWEEN A FIG TREE AND AN APPLE TREE; IT
begins in knowledge and ends in love, but there is also a paradise
to be kicked out of, and brokenness, suffering, and death, and then,
of course, there must be something born anew out of all that earth-
rattling change. Something glorious, or at least gloriously human.

And the climax must take place in Los Angeles, California, because
epics feel at home here. Epics and epicenters: on January 17, 1994, at
4:31 A.M., the Northridge Earthquake took hold of us and shook us
like infants, our heads snapping forward and back. No control. No
warning. That's how we woke in the thundering dark, my husband
and I howling in our bed because we believed we had awakened just
in time to see the walls of our house bury us.

But wait. I want to put the earthquake on hold a while, for when
it comes, there will be no stopping it. Better to begin this story in
the preceding autumn, when my husband, Phil, and I were married
between a fig tree and an apple tree, in the backyard of the rundown
bungalow we'd felt lucky to buy a few months earlier for fifteen,
maybe twenty, thousand dollars more than it was really worth. That's
what you do in Los Angeles—buy and hope, buy and hope, like
watching the hot yellow smog hanging over the San Gabriel Mountains meet the cool marine layer blowing in from Zuma Beach, and
calculating from that how long you can afford to live in such an in-
sane paradise of fire and flood, mud slide and earthquake, riot and
Republicans, bougainvillea and roses, roses, late into December. Back
east people say that there are no seasons here, but they are wrong. In

3

Los Angeles—El Pueblo de Nuestra Señora la Reina de Los Angeles, as the Spanish settlers lovingly crowned it in 1781—my favorite season, autumn, comes dry and hot and smelling of eucalyptus bark curling from the trees; after ten years of living here I have learned to look carefully for that season's signs, like a jeweler squinting through her loupe to detect a diamond's glitter and flaws.

Phil and I were married on just such a sultry day, Halloween eve, 1993. The idea to throw the wedding ourselves had the cockeyed logic of a Judy Garland–Mickey Rooney movie: You make the stage! I'll make the costumes, and my kid brother can sell lemonade! It was about that naive. Two days before the wedding, superheated Santa Ana winds blew in from Death Valley as we maniacally enlisted out-of-state relatives to help us finish painting crumbling stucco, hoping especially to cover cracks along the house's foundation, where forty-five years of plate tectonics had wreaked their own small havoc ("*Cosmetic* cracks," the appraiser assured us when we took our first, skeptical, look at the place). The backyard, which for years had featured nothing but ancient, dried dog shit and parched hardpan crisscrossed by mini–fault lines, now sported a virgin crop of emerald rye grass, untouched. We didn't dare walk on the fragile seedlings we had been watering obsessively for weeks—that was being saved for the big day.

We had managed, however, to trim the long-neglected fig tree, one of the few established plants in the backyard. It stood hunched in the southeast corner like an oversized child conscribed to repeating the fourth grade again and again: it bore Mission figs like big, black teardrops long after its growing season had ended. Fully ripe, the figs began to resemble hand grenades exploding of their own sweetness; ruby split seams drew long battalions of ants into the branches. But when the drying would begin, signaling the inevitable fall, the fruit drooped like a woman's breasts sucked in after many years of childbirth and nursing.

Our yard smelled permanently fermented, oversweet with fig wine. Phil and I hooted when we saw the enormous leaves the tree produced. Looking at each leaf's long, phallus-shaped middle bract, we understood why the fig leaf was the perfect post-Eden cover-up—for Adam, that is. Poor Eve would have found plenty of coverage, but no form-following-function for her. I imagined a sloppy leaf bikini, always slipping out of her hands, maybe stuck on with a glue of mashed

DOROTHY BARRESI

fruit and spit. It didn't seem fair to me that Eve had had so much to hold in place, and so much more to cover up.

But where, you ask, is the apple tree? It's right there, in our next-door neighbors' yard, growing on the other side of the redwood fence that separates their astonishingly tidy lawn from our ramshackle place. We had first spied the Johnsons' Elysium—they are Max and Betty to us now, dear ones—the old-fashioned way, by peeking through a knothole. Surreptitiously we marveled at their pond and fountain, outbuildings painted in coordinating shades of pale green, and the raspberry bougainvillea spilling over perfectly placed trellises. Very Martha Stewart, we decided, but not fussy or put-offish. The branches of the apple tree were loaded down with Golden Delicious apples growing in the correct season. They hung over the fence as though ready to take our hands and pull us over to a cooler, better place. On our property the shade cast by this tree was pretty enough to call a bower. When Phil and I took our wedding vows in front of our friends and families—whose dress shoes were sinking all the while into two inches of emerald rye grass seedlings and soaked, unsteady earth—we stood midway between our fig tree and the shade of that apple tree: between all the dumb choices of the past and all our hard-won knowledge. Both Phil and I had, at our respective universities on separate coasts in separate acts of ignorance, managed to marry badly and divorce during graduate-school days. Now what we wanted most on that hot, windy autumn day five years ago—what we shall always want—was a green, growing place where we could stand together, knowing what we know. Or, I should say, knowing what little we can know.

And of course the sun was shining that day because this *is* a paradise, isn't it? Los Angeles. I remember Phil and I exchanging vows, shaking a little, and laughing, because the dozen champagne bottles the waiters had half-opened in anticipation of the best man's toast began exploding on their own from the heat. Everybody jumped. *Bam, bam, bam!* It sounded the way gunshots sound in the movies or on television news, where some hapless witness always begins his story this way: "At first I thought it was firecrackers."

When my father announced at the dining room table in 1954 that he intended to marry my mother, Mary Lenore O'Loughlin, of the Chicago, Buffalo, and Dublin O'Loughlins, his mother ran from the room crying, fist to her mouth. It didn't matter that my mother's family was every bit as Catholic as my father's family—indeed, she had a rather famous theologian on her side, one George O'Brien, plus a priest and a Dominican nun-in-training—or that she was from a prospering middle-class home, or that she was, as my Irish relatives would say, "a lovely person." She *wasn't* Italian; it was that simple. It couldn't work. But for forty-two years it did work, in its own crazy way. Behind my parents' backs I called them the Bicker Twins. The *Reader's Digest* version includes my father's overreaching perfectionism, his hot temper, his delightful affectionate streak, and his passion for knowledge and new experience that found form in countless hobbies taken up and dropped over the years—motorcycling, wine making, photography—to which my mother would raise one wry eyebrow, shake her head, then, smiling to herself, walk back to the kitchen, cigarette in hand.

I have a theory about this. For so many men of my father's generation, first marriages were acts of allowable rebellion in a mostly closed society; they wanted to choose someone as unlike their mothers as possible in order to make the break that would enable them to begin their own adult lives. My Grandmother Barresi was *echt*-Italian: exuberant and earthy, a nonstop talker, cook, and famously spoiling mother and housewife ("Ma—sit down and eat something for crying out loud" was the chorus heard at every meal laid out in my grandparents' house). That would explain, I think, my father's having fallen in love with my mother, with her Irish pride and fine manners, her sophistication, her sharp wit, her innate generosity counterbalanced by an emotional reserve and a penchant for a martyr's downcast solitude that enabled her to go someplace far into herself when necessary. From that distant vantage point she would look out at the chaos of our large family (at least two of the five children the direct result of the Catholic prohibition against any truly trustworthy birth-control method) and, as if stationed in a remote fire tower, watch for flames that meant she would have to come back to us, reluctantly, and put them out. "When you were all little," my mother told me once, "and there were at least two of you in diapers at any given time, I thought the only way out for me was suicide."

Coming home from school late afternoons, I often found my mother lying on the sofa napping, one hand covering her eyes. She would lift that hand slowly and smile a bit as I bumped and jostled my way into the darkened living room with my book bag and my stories of the day spent with the nuns of St. Sebastian and St. Vincent. Because I have always been what my mother would call "a real talker," having received that gene no doubt directly from my Grandmother Barresi, I loved entertaining her with my stories, but it was more than garrulousness that kept me talking. I wanted to draw my mother more fully into my life, and away from reticence. Was I a good daughter? Could I make her happy despite the hard life that had befallen her? How could I be sure? Always on those afternoons I felt awkward, and a little guilty, for having awakened her from her sleep.

Perhaps it was on one of those occasions that I first promised myself I would not have children of my own—well, maybe one, and only under ideal circumstances I could not then imagine. That feeling changed over the years, softened. By the time Phil and I fell in love, I allowed that somewhere in the distant, abstract future I might want to have a baby, but the truth is, motherhood terrified me. I understood too well that it was an unrelieved act of service; it had overwhelmed my mother, but it would not claim me. Many times I repeated that vow to myself in my younger years, but especially in the evenings, seated at the family dinner table, where my mother would push her food into small piles, sigh, light a cigarette. Sometimes she broke into tears as my brothers, sister, and I squabbled with one another over almost everything, including a second helping of some dish she hadn't quite made enough of. Then I'd feel that familiar panic wringing my gut. "You're making Mom cry," I'd yell. "Stop it." From a young age I remember watching my mother secretly to see if she was all right. Monitoring her. What were the signs of coming distress? How could I stave off her sadness—by what good act or joking diversion? Was there data I could collect to help predict when next the earth would open up and the darkness break loose across her face and I would find myself slipping into the crevasse after her, flailing, trying to grab her hand but never really holding her up?

After living in Los Angeles for ten years, I know this much about earthquakes: they come by wave and slip and thrust. They come when least expected, but once come, they bring the overwhelming knowledge that they should have been *constantly* expected—no, anticipated.

Silly me! I forgot that every foundation under me and every ceiling over me, every tree and root and anodized, postmodern, glass-walled skyscraper can shake loose and heave up and collapse and kill me flat in a finger snap—silly me!

How do we forget faults? Rock is sheared sideways at right angles. Waves move through the earth's crust and are reflected or refracted back, causing tremendous shaking intensities. There are blind faults and hidden faults. There is energy released in zones, some through rock, some through water. There are liquefaction and weak strata, foreshocks we shrug about, and slow, rolling aftershocks we doze through, lulled, as though the earth's magnificent growing pains were our very own cheesy-motel Magic Fingers.

Through water and surface rock and alluvium come the ruptures we always forget to expect. In this way, earth evolves. In the Santa Susanna Mountains, just a few miles northwest of where I live, Oat Mountain grew fifteen inches higher in the thirty seconds of the Northridge Earthquake. Valleys deepened and widened. Freeways buckled or uncoupled in great gaping holes: my living room is four feet closer to San Francisco now!

Strike-slip fault. Dip-slip fault. Reverse fault. Unknown fault—the fault responsible for January 17, 1994, was unknown until 4:31 A.M. of that day. Magnitude: 6.7. No warning. Now it has a name, the Oak Ridge Fault, which is said, like some California merlots, to have a complex and subtle character, not wholly understood, but clearly worthy of our consideration.

But what started it, you ask, this release of tremendous energy along an unknown fault line twelve miles below the place where we build our homes? Who knows? The earth's lithosphere supports both ocean and land. It is like a great desert tortoise's shell, if the distinctive markings on that shell were enormous plates, discrete, rubbing and bumping against each other over millions of years. Growing, grinding down, reconfiguring. And we ride on the back of that ancient creature, unaware of our destination, unaware most of the time that we are moving at all.

This is what I know about predicting earthquakes: precisely nothing.

On November 2, 1993, when Phil and I were on our honeymoon, my mother was diagnosed with lung cancer. She had been in pain for months. Had, in fact, been tested in Florida before setting out for southern California and the wedding, and initial results seemed good. There was talk of bursitis, an old complaint dating back to the days when she had endlessly carried a baby in one arm while holding back a toddler bent on mischief with the other. There was talk of cortisone shots; they had helped before. The cough she had lately developed might be a touch of pneumonia, a cold she hadn't quite been able to shake, and it was academic anyway: nothing, she had promised, would keep her from attending the wedding. But the morning after the ceremony, when Phil and I were stumbling around the house gathering up rented champagne flutes and trying to find room in the freezer for still more leftover wedding cake, my father showed up at the front door looking stricken. They were leaving for LAX within the hour, he said. The burning ache along my mother's shoulder blades and her deep, persistent cough had become unbearable. She was at the hotel packing and crying. She didn't want to come and say good-bye— didn't want to spoil things for us just as we were starting out.

Remorse rocked me. Why had I not seen what my mother, by long force of habit, had masked?

Now, talking with my parents from a faux-antique phone in the sitting room of a Napa bed-and-breakfast, I felt the dizzy sensation of falling. I was on the honeymoon so many Angelenos take, a dream tour north along Pacific Coast Highway's stunning cliffs. Cambria. Big Sur. Land's end. The winter ocean churned below us, with its purples and deep greens; it had never looked so beautiful or dangerous. I developed vertigo; by the second day I just couldn't look down. How was it possible that now, when we were safely inland surrounded by the soothing colors of autumn vineyards, I was falling for real, story after story, down through everything inside me? Phil held my hand.

"It's a primary tumor," my mother was explaining, far off. She had already adopted doctor-speak, that fact-based idiom we resort to when faced with the terrors of our own ungovernable bodies. It was not, she added, a metastasis of the breast cancer she had had, and presumably beaten, four years before. "That's a good thing," my father said a little too brightly when it was his turn to talk. "The oncologist is very hopeful. It's ground zero. We've still got lots of options."

In *Southern California: An Island on the Land,* Carey McWilliams celebrates the idiosyncrasies of a place that writers such as Joan Didion and Nathanael West paint darkly indeed. That explains, perhaps, why the book is well known in Los Angeles and nowhere else. In 1946, McWilliams parses the phrase "earthquake weather" from an Angeleno's point of view: "Most Southern California residents are thoroughly convinced...that earthquakes are invariably preceded by a period of what is called 'earthquake weather.' Despite the fact that earthquakes have occurred in summer, winter, spring and fall, the belief in earthquake weather persists. In the sense in which most residents understand the expression, 'earthquake weather' refers to a close, stifling, sunless, muggy day."

McWilliams, fan of the sweetly oddball and the outright weird, enumerates the many myths Angelenos have attached to earthquakes over the years, among them the notions that they can cause permanent menstrual irregularities (of course!), that an invalid suffering paralysis was once cured by a quake's vibrations, and that the Long Beach Earthquake was caused by a curse the Rev. Robert Schuller placed on southern California after he failed to be elected to the United States Senate. And, of course, there are cover-up theories, a lot like the ones I heard as a professor at California State University, Northridge, which sustained more damage on January 17, 1994, than any university had in the history of the United States. In that awful spring semester when we were teaching in trailers set up in camps around the toppled campus, earnest students reported that the government, in league with seismologists at Cal. Tech. and insurance companies in Sacramento, was withholding the truth about the Northridge Earthquake's real magnitude and death toll, and, indeed, about the probability of the *really* big one coming in the not-distant future, lest, I suppose, Angelenos started jumping off the very buildings they were now, dutifully, "retrofitting."

Last week, driving back from Home Depot with two more cans of Swiss Coffee flat interior latex paint for the never-ending renovation of our house, I asked Phil, born and raised in California, what the phrase "earthquake weather" meant to him. What did it *really* mean?

Phil paused for a moment to think. Naturally, I jumped in.

"*I* think," I said, "that it means that the weather is so nice here, so similar from one sunny day to the next that a little humidity and barometric pressure freaks everyone out. There has to be *something* to worry about. We're sure that some sort of cosmic tax is being levied against us for having enjoyed such a garden spot, and so many walk-around-in-your-shirtsleeves days. It's very Catholic, really. Enjoying yourself? Wham! How about the possibility of a nice 7.0 to remind you that it ain't all fun and games, baby. You play, you pay. But the thing is, earthquakes are like death—they come like a thief in the night. We don't know when one will hit. So we're desperate. And out of that desperation come bogus theories about the weather, or birds circling, or whatever. It's the *absence* of signs that we take for a sign, which is ludicrous. Earthquake weather is really all about knowing we can't know anything for sure. Nothing is what it seems."

Phil, whose Protestant ancestors left Spain for Finland during the Inquisition and who understood the virtue of keeping quiet, waited for me to finish, flicked on his blinker as we turned onto our street, and said, quietly, "No."

He waited another moment. "It isn't the absence of bad weather. Or retribution. Earthquake weather is weather that is so still and hot and uncomfortable that one feels, rightly or wrongly, that something bad is brewing. It's calm, but it's a disturbing calm. One intuits this—something isn't right."

There are two more details you should know before I let the Northridge Earthquake loose on Los Angeles (Can you feel how impatient it's gotten? How it keeps insisting on little narrative foreshocks to whet your taste for shaking?).

In mid-November 1993, two weeks after our honeymoon, when Phil and I were back home in Los Angeles working, living our lives, I got pregnant. By accident. I won't go into the exact physiological happenstance of our mistake; you've made love: you understand these things. Let's just say we were using barrier methods, and that somehow, the barriers came down. I was shocked and affronted: how could the universe fail to consult me on a matter that would change my life forever? *My* life. I wasn't ready. It wasn't the right time—I was due to take a sabbatical in the fall!

And this: by early January, after biopsies and radiation and the indignities of being tethered to an oxygen tank, my mother's hands began to tremble uncontrollably. She could barely raise a teacup to her mouth. Her left arm and leg started numbing. Her oncologist guessed what tests proved true: the cancer had spread to the brain, as lung cancer so often does.

To imagine what it felt like in Los Angeles on January 17th at 4:31 A.M., fill a shoe box with small bits of stone and earth and scrap metal and teeth and seashells. Cover the box, then shake it like hell. Feel that? That's what we were in. And for the record, the weather on the 16th was cool and blustery, the air clear, and the San Gabriel Mountains standing out in marvelous relief.

I heard it first, one second of monster thunder waking me. Then Los Angeles roared, all 465 square miles of it, shaking so hard that the four corners of our bedroom bucked and twisted out of plumb. "Earthquake," I shouted, grabbing onto Phil, who was also shouting. It was a matter of seconds. Desks and televisions, dishes and liquor bottles, books and bookcases and mirrors were falling and smashing in every room; we heard this as our bed slid across the floor. Phil tried to get up but was slammed back. The power lines outside our window arced and went dead.

For the first time in its history, all of Los Angeles went dark at once. Hollywood. Santa Monica. Watts. South Central. East L.A. Brentwood. Beverly Hills. The barrios of Pacoima. The malls of Sherman Oaks. Malibu. All the light pollution of our human lives extinguished.

It's likely, if you ask an Angeleno what she remembers most about that night, she will tell you about the darkness. Cold, brilliant winter darkness. When Phil and I were able to get outside, in the awful moments between the quake and its first frightening aftershock, we watched neighbors running out of houses with their children wrapped in blankets, and their dogs howling in the driveways, and every star in the heavens pressing down as if some membrane between us and the sky had been torn open and we were now part of infinite black space. Apocalypse—everyone I know had that thought cross their minds.

We got in our car and turned the radio on; we didn't dare go back into the house. The first reports were coming in, so we sat in our pajamas, shivering and listening as aftershocks bounced the car on its rubber tires. The baby in my belly gripped down and rode it out.

An hour later, between aftershocks (Cal. Tech. reported five thousand measurable aftershocks in the first thirty days alone following the Northridge Earthquake, an ongoing trauma that kept defeating our best efforts to put the disaster "behind us"), we managed to get back into the house. The shattered glass and toppled furniture made it rough going, but the phone was still working. I put a call through to my parents. My mother answered. She was already crying. "I've got Peter Jennings on the television. He said people were killed in an apartment in Northridge, and there's fires, and I was so scared for you and the baby. I just can't take any more." I heard her sobbing, then my father's strained voice picked up: "Hey, kid, you all right?"

When the oncologist discovered that the lung cancer had spread to my mother's brain, he gave her six months—though "gave" hardly seems the right word. And his prediction would be right, or very nearly, though I was sure then that he was wrong. Hadn't her color and her appetite improved since the radiation course had been completed? She was sleeping well, and her pain was medicated and under control. Sure, she had never gotten her full lung function back, and the oxygen machine was a nuisance, but death seemed a long way off. "I'm not going anywhere," she said. "Not until I see that baby of yours." For my part, I promised her that Phil and I would bring the baby to Florida as soon after the birth as possible. That's what I told her. That's what I believed.

But of course that's not what happened. Cancer is a force of nature, awesome and frightening as any flood or wildfire or earthquake or hurricane, though it works microscopically, cell by demolishing cell. No two cases are exactly the same—how could they be, when our bodies are so different, one from another? But medicine dwells in a deterministic world of probability and past behavior. Doctors knew well enough how to read the signs of my mother's case, though we, as usual, mistook them.

My mother died on June 25, 1994. I was eight months pregnant. When she died, skeletal and wracked, ancient at sixty-six, my father knelt by her bedside, and we all said a prayer of numb grief. How could she be gone? How could her own body, body that bore us, have risen up against her in such a way? My father and mother had argued almost to the end, but my father had nursed her with great tenderness, too. Now he told us that they had, on the first night of their honeymoon in the Pocono Mountains, knelt by the bed and said a prayer that their marriage would be blessed in God's eyes. He thought it was fitting that we pray by her bedside now, at the end of her life, and I believe he was right. For forty-two years she was wife and mother, not always happily, not always as we had wished or needed, but she had given her life to the task, and we loved her desperately for it.

After the wake and funeral, I went back to Los Angeles to prepare for the baby's arrival. But how? Everything around us seemed broken or tainted. In the quake's thirty seconds, sixty people had died, eleven thousand residences had been destroyed, 250 gas lines ruptured, nine highway overpasses snapped in half. A department store had collapsed, an aqueduct had broken open, parking garages and apartment buildings and hospital wings were crisscrossed with yellow tape or condemned outright. Thousands of the "new homeless" were still living in the four tent cities the Red Cross had erected—one just down the road from us. True, many things were not ruined—our little fixer-upper, for example, came through it all like a champ, with only "cosmetic damage along the foundation," in the words of our insurance woman. We had survived a natural disaster—the most costly in U.S. history—with our bodies and our house intact; we knew we had much to be thankful for, not the least of which was our son, soon to be born. But it was the things that had fallen in on themselves like so many overwrought wedding cakes that ruled our emotions.

It is normal, the experts say, for depression to follow catastrophic events. It can last for years. Six months after the Northridge Earthquake, Phil and I were still waking each night at 4:30 A.M., jittery and unable to sleep. We would lie in the dark, whispering or just holding hands. Were we really safe? Had we set aside enough water and batteries should another, larger quake hit? Was the nursery furniture secure? We ran through evacuation drills with contingency plans for every occasion. We imagined ourselves like Aeneas, fleeing a burning city with our son on our backs.

Money, too, was a worry. The earthquake had dealt a coup de grâce to a city that had already been weakened by recession and peacetime cuts in aerospace and defense contracts. My job was safe, but what about Phil's, tied as it was to "soft money" and state-government largesse? Worse, our house's value had plummeted thirty thousand dollars in one night! Our address was listed on an official map of earthquake danger zones, but we were no longer able to afford earthquake insurance. Would we ever be able to sell the place and move up? The

L.A. Times ran stories daily about the great exodus: Angelenos leaving in record numbers for Oregon and Washington. Paradise was lost, or else it had moved to the Great Northwest along with everyone else, and besides, hadn't moral decay, gang violence, and racial tension already spoiled the place? U-Haul couldn't keep enough trucks in the city. There were reports of increased rat infestation in the palm trees, mosquitos breeding in abandoned pools. Everyone, it seemed, was leaving L.A. or talking about leaving L.A.

On August 3, 1994, Dante Charles Matero was born, the most beautiful, magnificent human being on the planet.

He came to us on a day when the Santa Ana winds were blowing in off the desert, and temperatures reached 107 degrees. If these were signs of what lay ahead for us, Phil, Dante, and I, we didn't stop to read them. There was a baby to feed, a restless, magic life, and autumn was coming. The fig tree was weighed down with sweetness and ants, and the cracks in the stucco needed patching again. My mother had lain in the ground for less than two months. On a few occasions she came to me in my dreams. There, she was dead and alive at the same time—I could tell that it surprised her, and that she wanted to explain, and although I had a hundred questions, a baby crying like a wounded cat in the background would always interrupt us, and I would wake bleary-eyed and wanting and confused. The baby was mine. Love needed me. Love had made me over.

Some mornings, I was outside pushing the baby stroller by seven, stepping around the debris of fallen chimneys and cinder-block walls. Occasionally I would pass a workman climbing a ladder with a paintbrush or a load of mortar in his hand, and we would nod to each other, and smile.

WALKING AND

FALLING

DOUGLAS CARLSON

I

WE WERE WALKING ALMOST AS FAST AS WE COULD—TEN OF US,
single file. I was last. We walked single file because silver sage up to
five feet high enclosed the trail so narrowly that our shoulders, made
unnaturally wide by down-filled parkas, brushed sage leaves as we
passed by. We walked fast because the best part of the hike was over—
we had seen bighorn sheep—and because we had several miles to go:
through bottomland, then up and down some medium buttes to an
impossibly steep one at the trailhead. The sun setting, the wind howling, February in the North Dakota Badlands.

I hope I never get used to sage. It has come to define the West for
me the way cowboy hats, longhorn cattle, or rodeos do for others.
So I was thinking about sage. (Anyone who has hiked a narrow trail
purposefully for a time long enough to memorize the entire posterior
of the person directly in front knows how this mind traveling goes.)
I was remembering an old TV western I watched as a little kid. *Sagebrush Trail*. Probably one of the first television westerns made. It came
on around supper time. All I can remember for sure is the opening: a
grainy sketch of some southwestern landscape, the show's title in a
"western" script, and a voice-of-God voice-over who stretched out
the words in a thrilling way. SA-A-A-GE BRUSH TRA-AA-IL-L-L.
The "trail" trailed away. This was in upstate New York in the 1950s.
What a stupidly precise memory—if accurate at all. I suspect that I
thought sagebrush was saguaro cactus, or maybe it referred to the entire landscape pictured, like "grasslands" or "outback." Sagebrush.

Now, after decades of hikes in northeastern fields and woods, here I was nearly surrounded by the stuff. I love how from a distance it makes huge areas of flatland seem even flatter. I love how its color can't quite be pinned down: gray, silver, purple. I love how even in winter you can grab a leaf, crush it in your hand, sniff, and wake up your senses all over again. I did that.

Then I fell.

We learn things with our bodies too. I've heard it called "haptic sense." It teaches things like steepness and traction. It taught me about sage: pretty at the top, tough and strong below. My toe had caught a low branch growing out over the trail. I thought I could kick through it, but I couldn't. One of the things my mind (haptic sense) screamed at me as I pitched forward was "witch's hobble." This useless bit of input referred to moose wood, or hobblebush, a plant, legend has it, notorious for tripping up hikers in northeast woods—1,500 miles away, another fall. Another dumb thing it told me was to avoid, no matter the cost, falling into sage. So I became as narrow as possible by hugging myself and fell flat—with my right elbow directly beneath my rib cage.

A week or so later I was still walking with pain but mobile enough to celebrate a signal day—the first with a windchill above freezing—by walking along the Red River of the North. I saw two or three juncos, heard chickadees singing territorial songs, and saw two Canada geese in open water on the North Dakota side of the river. The usual house sparrows chattered and crows called—an average day of birding for Moorhead, Minnesota, in late winter. The air was forty degrees, no wind. A week earlier the air was five degrees, wind north-northwest at twenty-two miles per hour, windchill was minus thirty-four.

When my wife and I returned to Minnesota after our semester break back east, a stretch of six days began when the windchill never went above zero. On January 9th the air was minus seven, the wind twenty-one m.p.h., and the windchill minus fifty. That afternoon I saw sun dogs—parhelion—for the first time. By the next day the windchill was minus fifty-seven. It's all in my notes. Okay, I did get a bit obsessed with weather. But this was my first winter on the prairie, and my friends kept saying, "This is nothing. We'll go a couple weeks when the air temp never goes above zero. You should have seen last year."

Last year.

And there, walking and thinking in Gooseberry Park, Moorhead, Minnesota, I suddenly had a weather memory of a year before. The parking lot of Jamestown, New York, General Hospital. I'm walking toward my younger sister who's just come from the airport. The sun is shining. We're in shirtsleeves. We hug. I say, "Honey, I'm sorry. You missed him by a half-hour." "Oh damn." And we hug and cry a little bit there in a deceptive, late-winter sun.

A year before my walk and fall, my father died. I hope not to be judged for not remembering the exact date; sentimentalism was something we weren't brought up around, and knowing the anniversary date of a death just never occurred to me. Or someone, well meaning, might say, "It was as if he told you to go out and walk that day." Well, yes, in the sense that he taught me to go whenever possible where nonhuman things live and to see what they were up to. And winter had been long and strange. I had learned about fauna from behind windows in the frozen, northern plains suburbs: that house sparrows fed on the undersides of cars, that cottontails ate their own shit, and that crows scavenged Hefty bags on trash pickup day. I longed for spring.

Suddenly I was drawn back to the wonderful, false-spring world of melting snow and bubbling streams and pussy willows, of walks through the woods near my boyhood home in upstate New York. My father believed he was a dowser, a water witch. Odd that a physicist would think that he could become a medium for the presence of water, but I remember watching in amazement as he would walk a field, forked apple bough in his hands, and the stick would suddenly begin to tremble, then point directly down. To water, he said—although I don't remember whether any wells were actually dug at his recommendation. But I do know that I could feel water move under snow. In that slack season before the color returned—red of trilliums, yellow of adder's-tongue—I walked the woods with a maple sapling pole searching out the rills that began in secret places under the snow and ran to buried gullies and ditches. To free their water, I poked holes in the snow until it weakened and fell into the water, turned silver, and disappeared. The water took on the color of the leaves it flowed over, leaves rank with life, washed by the first water of spring. They grew richer and darker before my eyes as I worked to create wider and fuller streams. In the end, the woods would be filled with the bubble, tone, and splash of open water, and I would walk happily home. My mind was full of these memories.

Then I fell.

The Red River, as it loves to do, had gone a bit above flood stage a couple days before. Before it receded, some water had frozen on the riverbanks. Two inches of snow had fallen, hiding the slope of ice. Walking with my hands in my pockets, thinking of my father, and listening to the chickadees' spring songs of rebirth—I never had a chance.

He never had a chance either, the first time I saw him fall. It was typical of the terrifying scenes that he would have to somehow accustom himself to. Or maybe he already had. It had been nearly twenty years since a concerned nurse, who happened to be on a Holland tulip tour with my parents, watched my father get on the tour bus then took my mother aside and used the word that would control the rest of her life with my father: "Parkinson's." Those were years of tests and diagnoses and misdiagnoses, fear and hope, and then the inevitable truth that life would be measured, from then on, by the spaces of time between falls. I had heard about them, and I knew they were more frequent than anyone thought. One day when I was visiting, he motioned me over to his chair. He pulled back his shirt cuff so I could see a blood-soaked handkerchief; then he showed me the abrasions underneath. "Don't tell your mother," he whispered.

This first fall that I saw happened in the bathroom of a small cottage my wife and I were renovating. I was putting in a new toilet; he was watching, leaning on his cane. Suddenly he lurched forward, spun around nearly 360 degrees, and crashed to the floor. I can look at this now in different ways.

This is what happened. As I was bending over, carefully fitting a beeswax collar, which would keep the toilet from leaking, over the drainpipe, and as a cool northwest breeze blew off Lake Erie and through the bathroom window as it often does after a low-pressure system passes, one area of my father's brain, the substantia nigra, tried to send a message to another area, the striatum, which controls movement, balance, and walking. The message making this synaptic connection is generally aided by a chemical substance called dopamine.

My father had an abysmal supply of dopamine; the message never got there.

Or a son watched his father fall violently and helplessly to the floor. His attempts to catch him, to break the fall, came too late. In that moment, the father has failed the son; the son has failed the father. Nothing between them will ever be the same. They know their roles in the endless chain of dying fathers and helpless sons.

Or something incomprehensible and powerful visited us there. What do you say to something that can inexorably transform a large and strong man into a pallid, comma-shaped thing lying on white sheets and breathing oxygen from a machine? And what secrets does this power whisper to you as it freezes your limbs rigid, turns your brain upside down inside your head, and throws you to the ground again and again?

But before I thought to ask my father questions like that, he lost his speech. For a while we could ask questions like "Do you want apple or grape juice?" and figure out the word that came out. Then we learned to ask only yes-or-no questions. The last complete sentence I remember him saying was one day when I was helping him into the car. He got down and inside okay, but his right leg just wouldn't follow him in. I finally picked it up and over the doorsill. He looked at the leg as if it were a failed part of a flawed machine. "I'm no good," he stuttered.

The number of falls increased as did the broken bones: wrist, hip, back. Secondary symptoms arrived and stayed. And finally he was immobile and silent. He could chew and swallow. Then he could swallow only. Then he couldn't do that.

11

Any place can become a home place. To revisit is to attend a family reunion, a wedding, a wake, to wander through old stories while making new ones. We came to Cape Cod in 1965, when its fringes and the people who lived there were still more or less untamed. My father's brother, Alden, who owned a cottage colony in North Truro, invited us the first time; he embodied Cape Cod for us—spontaneous, brooding, sometimes dangerous—the antithesis of my father and his safe, inland home. Both were my teachers, the only teachers that I recall.

Except for a grieving period after Alden's death—when the land was no good without him—we've been coming back every year since.

But home can change. We change. The land changes. Our changes decide for us how we see, changing the land again. And although we choose to overlook the fact, we effect change. We moan about the tourists, often using the word "hordes." We are, of course, part of each year's horde.

Our stories, we remind ourselves, are a constant. But I'm not so sure anymore...

—Remember when the kids were small and we had that huge beach fire and someone called the fire department?

—Was that both kids, or was Jeffrey too young?

—It had to be both because we were staying at Chase's.

—No, wasn't it in the place right on the edge? The one they moved?

—We'll have to ask Kevin if he remembers.

—He was too young. He'll just remember the story we told him.

—He'll remember.

—Come to think of it, did someone actually call the fire department, or were we just worried that someone would?

...and so on until the story and all its (mis)information is finally reconstructed.

Furthermore, each year that we return to Cape Cod deepens the sense of loss: of undeveloped space, familiar places, former certainties, life itself I suppose. Each year it worsens; time and people and places swirl in confusion. We hope for clarity, but we live as though we're late for some appointment. Only the hopelessly sedentary practice of lolling in the sun gives the illusion of peace. But it is an illusion at best, and besides, the sun doesn't shine all the time. Instinctively this last year, we fought back. My wife had her camera—gathering images to compare with images she had collected over the last three decades. I planned a hike.

The cottage we had stayed at for twenty years had stood with a half dozen just like it that were scattered among the dunes and hollows at the end of a sand cul-de-sac called Longstreet Lane (named after a sunken Liberty Ship whose disintegrating bones are still visible out in the bay). The cottage was a remnant of those common when we came to the Cape the first time: two tiny bedrooms, galley kitchen, living room, deck. This season's shock was the appearance of two huge houses on the lane. Our new neighbors had more bathrooms than we had rooms, self-important facade details that brought to mind small-town banks, thousands of dollars of glass to satisfy each room's demand for a water view, and endless protuberances: decks, porches, piazzas, verandas, widow's walks.

We found the second shock written under a map in a real estate brochure. "Four level, open lots, steps to Cape Cod Bay in Kingsbury Beach area, deeded beach rights. $149,900 each." On the map, the lots radiated from a cul-de-sac at the end of Cranberry Circle, a road that doesn't exist yet but soon will replace a wild place of bearberry, oak, bobwhites, and prairie warblers. It will intersect with Bayberry Avenue, another street that doesn't exist but is clearly Longstreet Lane; they either didn't care enough to get the name right or simply decided to rename it. Whatever. The rate of change, and its startling intensity, was changing.

The night before my hike, we woke up to watch the moon set on Cape Cod Bay—another constant. It was low tide. The flashes of the warning buoy at the remains of the *Longstreet* floated above a wash of yellow on the water that narrowed to where the sandbars began, then dispersed, then disappeared. Far offshore, a boat went about its business, the rumble of its motor hovering in the dark. Two octaves higher, another buoy somewhere sang. We counted to twelve. It sang again. And small waves broke over all the shorelines of all the sandbars. We carried these sounds into sleep and were startled awake a half-hour later. A woman screamed—high, sharp, inarticulate, terrified. We went to the phone, hesitated. Then another scream: "No. No. Please." A car door slammed, and a car drove away. Lights came on in one of the giant houses across the lane. We, our cottage, Cape Cod became suddenly urbanized. On many levels, nothing would be the same.

In the fall of 1988, I was drawn to explore the Nauset Plain that Henry Thoreau walked with Ellery Channing around 1850. Thoreau's Nauset was a bleak and treeless pile of sand and scrub; in 140 years mine had grown to a mature woods within the Cape Cod National Seashore. My recollections of that day remain vivid. Following a power line cut, I happened upon a path that took me deep into a woods of locust, pitch pine, and oak until I realized that the sound in the background was the ocean, and I began to notice the change in the trees from sedate and parklike to battered and twisted, then finally to scrub oak and pitch pine stunted by salt air, then a wind-blasted highland, a narrowing path, and suddenly the beach fifty feet below me and the Atlantic, blue before me to the limit of my vision. The experience moved me enough that I wrote a small essay that has served me well as a convenient container for an event I occasionally revisit in memory. So remembering that hike, or remembering the essay that recalled it—whether once or twice removed—I set out to reconstruct it.

From the start I was nudged by change. Where I had flushed a covey of bobwhite ten years before, I dodged cyclists, joggers, inline skaters, and even an inline cross-country skier on the new Cape Cod Bike Trail. But I gained the wood's edge and found the trail, or what I thought was the trail. A mile into the hike, my memory of the woods was shaken by some cleared land that I spotted through the trees to the south. I recalled hearing shotgun blasts during the earlier hike and finding a fork in the trail that took me away from the skeet-shooting range I knew was out there somewhere. But I couldn't find the fork, and instead of shotguns I began to hear hammering and radio music— the unmistakable sounds of a crew roofing a house. Then, after another mile or so, the trail opened up to a sand road, tire tracks, an abandoned truck transmission, and I realized my mistake: another trail, my old trail, ran parallel to this one. I backtracked, and walked north along the woods' margin until I found another break in the trees. I hadn't walked more than fifteen minutes before I knew I was on the right track; the memories came back clearly.

The landscape came back. The essay came back. I heard the birds and saw the trees. The trail led through the woods that I had recalled: oaks and kinglets, moss and leached sand. It leaned away from the skeet club. Traffic sounds from Route 6 faded, and surf sounds returned. I felt the same sense of anticipation as before when the woods shrank around me, fresh salt air touched my face. And I stood like some sort of speechless, wonder-struck devout at the edge of the Atlantic. Through more than a decade of change, the ocean, of course, remained the ocean, and my response to it remained primal. I stood and let all the reverence I could summon up be drawn from me. Then

I nodded to the sea and began to follow a path south along the crest of the bluff.

The path was a couple feet wide and hemmed in mostly by scrub oak and chokecherry up to five feet high. The shoreline and beach were obscured from me. Then suddenly another opening, and I looked out on the water, down on the beach. Directly below me was a ring of chicken-wire fence, about ten feet in diameter, that enclosed a rock and a few tufts of beach grass. In the middle, in the bull's-eye, sat a piping plover on its nest.

Change has come too quickly for the piping plover as well. Beach buggies, shoreline development, and new recreational demands appeared overnight by a shorebird's clock—no time to evolve an arrangement safer than laying eggs in a depression on an open beach. In 1986, the Fish and Wildlife Service listed the piping plover as a threatened species: a species likely to become "endangered," the final official stop before extinction. And although compromises have been struck and numbers have improved (there were eighty-three nesting pairs at the Cape Cod National Seashore in 1995), the debate over recreational access to the outer beach has been acrimonious. A frequently seen bumper sticker on ORVs—"Piping Plovers Taste Like Chicken"—reveals an almost perfect disdain for the natural world while unconsciously insinuating, by turning something wild into something domestic, the historical reason for this disdain: since Europeans settled New England, nonhuman living things have been reduced to commodities divinely placed on earth for our amusement or profit.

While I was standing on the bluff, thinking about plovers and bass fishing and ORVs, I was gazing through binoculars—at far-off ships, at the surf line, at a scoter offshore that I couldn't specify—trying to pull it all in, within reach. I came back to the plover just as it got up, walked to the edge of its enclosure, and slipped through to the world of "self-contained vehicles." I checked the nest—four eggs. From somewhere in its camouflaged world (protection from me, not underinflated ORV tires), a mate appeared, entered the enclosure, and began to incubate. I worked the metaphor: the last two weeks, the last thirty-five years, all reduced to a managed plover nest on a remote beach. The more the pieces fit into place, the scarier it all became.

I thought about one of my favorite places, the Badlands of the Theodore Roosevelt National Park in western North Dakota. A dirt road leaves the paved loop of the park's south unit and climbs through fields of short-grass prairie bordered on the west by two ridges and on the east by scattered, steep buttes. This is the best place in the park to watch pronghorns and to find coyotes during the day. One or two big bison always hang out in the buttes. Drive far enough on this road and you come to a thicket of ash and chokecherry that offers birds at any season: juncos and chickadees in the winter, northern yellow-throats and lazuli buntings in summer. And hard by the thicket is the fence that keeps the rest of the world from this tiny wild area, a sturdy fence more than six feet tall. A cattle grate crosses the road where "wild" ends and ranching begins.

Then I thought about a brief time my wife and I lived in a gated community. At first we found the gatekeepers intrusive, but we learned to love the peaceful and safe night walks, the fresh morning air from ground-floor windows left open all night.

And, of course, I thought about Cape Cod itself. A couple generations of us learned wildness there. We echoed Thoreau, "It is a wild rank place, and there is no flattery in it." And we loved the Cape for that fact. We left our northeastern towns and cities and found a place where humans didn't cast the final and deciding vote. Well, no longer.

The edge of a bluff is an invitation to fall. But I backed away instinctively and walked inland as I had done ten years before, over the same trail of stories and memories that brought me there. As I recited the details of what I had seen and heard, I felt as though my walking had somehow become a home place itself, the only one left after the real thing has been taken away, fenced off, subdivided, and sold.

III

Five months after my father died, two months after we sold the house and land and helped my mother settle into her apartment, my wife and I moved to the northern plains, the flattest land I had ever seen. Two months after that, I lost my balance. The first attack came in the middle of the night. I woke up on my back with the sensation that the inside of my head was being shaken violently while the outside remained unmoved. I called out to my wife who could only watch as I struggled to get up, then lurched around the room. As quickly as it came, the sensation disappeared, leaving me small and afraid. I looked out over our backyard, past the streetlights, toward the prairie—probably searching for the comfort of a flat horizon line. But my view was obstructed by the manic lines of contemporary suburban architecture, the endless energy and motion of peaks and valleys, angles and synclines. I tried to imagine the flat and immense acres of sugar beets and wheat that I knew rested in the darkness beyond the development where we lived. But the physical memory of imbalance was still in control. We went back to bed, turned on the television, and, sitting up, watched the Weather Channel until dawn. I concentrated on the logic of high and low pressure, isobars, and dew points. And I fought back memories of my father and the falls I watched him endure.

My problem turned out to be minor, and my health care—diagnosis, treatment, and cure—was flawless. For a month, I couldn't tip my head back to read the call letters on a top-shelf library book, I couldn't shoot a basketball, I slept sitting up. But my imbalance, an inner ear problem, called positional vertigo, was righted. And I was left on my own to wonder at the paradox of vertigo and prairie—and at another: of rebirth, the dead father, and the living son.

The writer Kent Meyers grew up in south-central Minnesota, a land of some of the flattest cultivated field in the country. But in *Witness of Combines* he writes: "[I] never understood the essence of the northern prairie, or felt its deepest power, until I went to the source of its story. At the border of Minnesota and North Dakota, near Moorhead and Fargo, lies the most minimalist of all possible landscapes, a place with which not even the simplicity of the sea can compete, a place where flatness has been perfected." This is where my wife and I arrived in the summer of 1997: at a land forever divided into squares, one mile to a side, bordered by gravel roads and planted to wheat, soybeans, sugar beets, corn; a land of pickup trucks that travel these roads on plumes of dust, never touching the ground; a land that immediately told me: "You are self-contained. Supply your own resources—your strength, your invincibility, your gravity." I thought of Thoreau, his walk over the length of Cape Cod, and his astonishment at the flatness of the sandy and treeless Nauset Plains. With no object to measure by, a solitary traveler "loomed like a giant." I was one of those giants, the tallest object on the landscape. Vulnerable, barely touching the earth. And surrounded by a featureless, treeless nothing. A searching eye may be drawn to a farmer's shelterbelt, perhaps a grain elevator. But these are too distant and remote to share the land with. In winter the shelterbelt shimmers above the land; elevators float over the wheat fields whose grains they hold. They might as well be high cold stars. And I walked on top of a flatness that even flatlander Meyers called "shocking."

Open, flat land turns you in on yourself. Sherwood Anderson: "A night on the prairie takes the shrillness out of men. They learn the trick of quiet." *Western Characters* author John McConnell: "[P]ioneers became more meditative, abstracted, taciturn."

The power of the prairie is that it silences you; it's a perfect place to grieve. Not codependent, public grieving, leaning on custom or community—this is pure inside stuff. Stand up on the prairie and you're, at once, giant and puny. You're alive, and your father's dead. And you, of course, are dying.

My father believed he was a dowser; he also believed some part of him would survive his own death. The paradox of rebirth. He believed a lot of crazy stuff. So did I; he was my teacher. Then I fell—into memory and home. And I think I know where it all began.

IV

On maps, it is Pilgrim Heights or High Head, but for us it was just The Hill. Cresting it, we saw the colors blown eastward across the bay. All the blues of Robert Motherwell's Provincetown palette streamed into our faces, then the yellow kitchen table in the beach house and, hanging by the door, the yellow oilskins that we wore on the beach rainy nights looking at the lights: blinking red, white, green. And we looked at the sea beyond the white of breaking waves to the darkest places. We were hermit crabs crawling into a shell, following its canals deeper and darker. It was like coming home.

The permanent part of Cape Cod—the land—ends at High Head between Truro and Provincetown. Old marine scarps here are the last rock on the Cape; then the land turns to sand that pulls you down, shifts beneath your feet, covers your tracks. It clarifies your human condition. I felt that strongest at Sea Song, the cottage colony that my Uncle Alden owned that was our first home on Cape Cod. A frequent memory of Sea Song even now is the feel of sand underfoot on the kitchen floor. We sat at night, rain and sand howling outside, while we drank coffee and talked. Always the sand grated under our feet—wet and cold and coarse. Sea Song lived in sand, shifted with it, was filled with it. Living in a world of sand and water, we sensed how alike they are. When we walked at night—on the flats at low tide, our foot bottoms felt the ripples of sand; on the ocean beach at Highland Light, we heard the bluff crumble away in miniature waterfalls of sand. And everywhere, sand purled and eddied, crowding us in. It climbed the porch and crept inside the door, teeming like ghost crabs under our feet, reminding us that a beach and a dark ocean waited beyond the wall and that the wall was thin.

In the months after he died, I had a strange recurring dream about my uncle. We were sitting at the table in front of the big upstairs window, looking across the bay to Provincetown. Suddenly the Pilgrim Tower collapsed. We saw men falling, business suits still buttoned, ties flying straight up. Women fell, skirts blowing clear of their scissoring thighs, arms thrown back. The tide was out, and the entire scene sank from sight into the wet sand of the tidal flats. I still believe that this wasn't my uncle reaching back from death to tell me something I needed to know. It was the sand and water reminding me that I was falling toward him.

There are two seasons on Cape Cod: life and death. The season of life, the season of color, lasts until the marsh and beach grasses turn brown and the clouds take over. From November to March, browns and grays sulk during the brief daytime and are blown away by the cold night sea winds. To survive, we have to find life in darkness until the color returns.

Cape Cod winter: a colorless daylight where the warmest place is also the darkest. In the accumulation of shadows under a spindled oak, in the heat living in the cells of dead grasses, in darkness, we remember how it feels to be warm: and a featureless night, when sea, sky, and land blend, interrupted only by the turn of a wave, the blink of a lighthouse beam.

After my uncle died and the family sold Sea Song, I came back to the Cape after it had emptied out. February. A good grieving month, maybe the best, because of what it offers and, ultimately, denies. Earlier in the day, I had driven in sunshine to the top of The Hill. Blue cut memories through the car window and into my eyes: the beach house, the upper room, the slant of light on the wall, and the waves outside the open door forever. Then clouds returned, and I spent the rest of the day in gray and brown. At Race Point, I endured as much of the beach blast as I could; then I bought a sandwich and retired to Nauset Light to watch for night. Through binoculars, I saw a loon diving for its supper. I tried to imagine going down, deeper and darker, finding something, then turning up to see the light air above. Each time the loon dove, I concentrated on its dive—deeper, darker, then up to light. But as night came on, the horizon line blended water and sky into the gray just before black. I lost sight of the loon and gave up trying to see anything on the water as the loon might have given up when, turning upward from its dive, it saw no light to swim toward.

The beam from the lighthouse made its circle, repeating the waves' rhythm, and I left the car to walk to the bluff's edge. It was as though I were waiting for my uncle to help me, but it was my own voice I heard: a step one way is to risk a fall into winter, but a step in the other direction can tilt the entire hemisphere toward the sun. Mine is no special case: I've been falling ever since.

BLACK BRANCHES

TAKING ON SNOW

PEGGY SHUMAKER

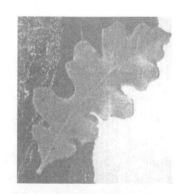

IN MARCH, IN FAIRBANKS, HARD WINTER'S USUALLY JUST ABOUT done. Ever since winter solstice, Interior Alaska has been gaining six or seven minutes of daylight every twenty-four hours. Gone are the brief days when the sun barely creeps over the lip of the horizon, limps along for three hours and change, and then dives back behind the earth's curve. Yet to come, in a month or two, the grand symphony of breakup, when grinding and heaving groans explode into the cannon fire of ice cracking. River ice changes every day, from a hard white highway to a nearly solid mosaic of white and turquoise. That shifts to jostling keyholes of deep black-green, widening as the river opens. Low, marshy spots still ice over at night, then melt into silty pools of celadon green. Soon we'll hear throaty Vs of Canada geese. Thin rafts of sandhill cranes will plummet feet first into barley fields next to Creamer's Dairy. But not quite yet.

In March, catkins swell and willows redden, knowing it's almost time to burgeon. People who have wintered over cut switches of red willow and bring them inside. Arranged in tall vases of warm water, cut branches believe they've made it through to another season, and unfurl the first leaves of spring within cabin walls. In March, people who have made it through hard cold break out of lethargy. Classical cross-country skiers set tracks for fifty miles and more around town, freed finally from the few lighted loops on campus or at Birch Hill. Telemark tracks fan like shoots of wild iris, splayed up open hillsides. Skiers squint behind high-tech sunglasses, grin into the glare, and stay out until the feeling fades in their fingertips and they have to spin their arms like whirligigs to force blood back into closed-off capillaries.

Cabin dwellers in March haul extra water, filling five-gallon jerry cans. Some drive out to the natural spring at Fox because that water tastes so good; others just fill up at the laundromat, where they take their showers while the dryers tumble. For the first time since the snow flew, they mop the place by the door where people kick off their Sorels, and balance the pulled-out felt liners on top to dry. Cabin dwellers sprinkle lime in their outhouses, as aromas return to the Far North. It's harder to split firewood now than it was at twenty below when rounds of birch jumped apart at each solid whack of the ax. But sun on stiff muscles feels so fine, March is a good time to split and stack a cord or two.

As the temperature edges up toward zero, whatever people have held back all winter rushes to the surface. Early leads in the ice along the Chena crack and widen just enough to tempt the first crazed kayakers to dare each other out on the water. They paddle till the ice crushes too close, taking care not to pinch their boats between shifting floes. Every spring, some dumb snow machiner skipping over overflow falls through the ice. Most years, witnesses on shore pull the guy, dripping and hypothermic, back to solid ground.

In March, some people who have wintered over break out of their lethargy into darkness, not light. What returns to them (or what they return to) is the blighted awareness that they've gone nowhere for another very long winter, and though the light should be making things easier or better, nothing's easy, nothing's better. Full dark induces a sloth life, physically, emotionally, spiritually, for all of us. For those who hole up with a bottle or who fight cabin fever by closing down bars, sun sparking off snow hurts. Whatever sorrows stalk the saddest among us take too much energy to deal with in deep winter. But in March, the sky's unbearable brightness stretches waking pain beyond endurance. The suicide prevention line puts on extra volunteers but can't stop the annual ritual of despair, renewed.

We fight back with the tools we have—friends, music, shelters and counselors, churches, full-spectrum light bulbs, potluck dinners. The military bases, full of folks far from friends and family, run special "survival" courses that do not involve cutting snow blocks to create an arctic shelter or how to set a wire snare. No, these classes involve rekindling the most elemental human fire—the desire to keep the flame flickering.

And still. And still one March the caribou change their migratory pattern. Troopers along Parks Highway have to direct traffic around the milling haunches and clattering snap hooves. Three caribou stand their ground near the top of the hill, smack in the middle of the lane leading to my log house. I watch the one with just one antler, knowing it's a buck, knowing that males lose their antlers first. Unbalanced, the remaining antler trails a little shred of last year's velvet, an unlikely survivor of long winter. Gravid or nursing females hold their antlers later into spring, needing them to defend patches of browse, hoof-scraped lichens, or the first tatters of caribou lettuce. Suffused with curiosity and peace, I look on. And as I watch the ancient migration stepping through the present and into the future, a young woman's life is ending. This is not an abstraction. I will not find out until the next morning, but eight miles away, in daylight turned dark, rage over-whelms one man. Still unsolved is the case of a young Alaska Native woman found raped and shot, left dead but still bleeding in the bath-tub of a dormitory. Troopers believe her attacker did not know Sophie Sergie, had no idea of her dreams or desires, but that he did harbor an immense hatred of women, and a violence too large for his strong body to contain. Unsolved, why a person people had to see but could not recall, a person so ordinary he was unremarkable, not out of place, a person capable of the most brutal devastation passes unnoticed among us. In smaller doses, what he carries, what he represents, surges within us. But we also carry what Sophie did—unrealized promise, curiosity about the wider world, and a finite time here on earth. I think of Sophie Sergie, this step in her journey done, and vacillate among anger, sorrow, fear, and a need to know. That night, for the first time in Alaska, I lock my door.

Extremes force us to treasure what's soon gone, to recognize our small place in the vast expanse. Heading up one March to Circle Hot Springs, we show off to guests from Arizona. Clear and sun dazzled, the sky is so full of itself, not one cloud streaks pure blue. We drive north out of Fairbanks to Eagle Summit, miles above the tree line, where we can turn a 360 and gaze on white hillsides stretching from under our boot soles to the jagged horizon, all around us evidence of what we'll never know. We breathe in that crystalline certainty of all we'll never fathom, bundle back into our small sphere of warmth, and drive on over gravel road that's much better frozen than it is thawed. One hundred miles short of the Arctic Circle, we soak in a huge swimming pool fed by natural hot springs. Early travelers who thought they were farther north misnamed this place, where modern adventurers pour buckets of hot water over the diving board so their feet won't stick. It's just cold enough for frost to form on our lashes and brows when we float, and for our hair to take on the sheen of polar ice caps. When the ache sets in, we duck underwater, reveling in the peculiar freedom of being outside and unencumbered by fleece and down for the first time since September. Heading back to town, mellow, we run into snow, not enough to worry about, but some. For reassurance, we point out to our friends the edge markers, huge lucky sevens with fluorescent orange tips we can sight to make sure we stay on the road. As the whirling soup thickens, Tito videos the whiteout. Lupita is not amused, and sets up a mantra: "Oh God, we're all gonna die. Oh God, we're all gonna die." Joaquin, usually chipper and vocal, stops asking us trivia questions from his political flash cards—"What is Pat Nixon's real first name? Give up?...Thelma!"

No one advises stopping in whiteout. The next car could ram us over the cliff, or the snowplow could crush our car like a recycled pop can. So we crawl along, eyes straining to catch the next orange marker before we lose sight of the one we can see. And as Lupita, eyes closed, gathers her son onto her lap, I begin to think about what it would mean if we were to die here, now, before what we like to think of as "our time":

Wide Icy River

How, driving in whiteout
    above tree line the summit
        road washed white blue-white
            gone to swirling powder, we gasp
                whirling inside the frosted sigh

of the earth.
    Straining in whiteout
        our eyes the eyes of creatures

                    unsuited to this element
                             vestigial, liquid ornaments

splashing for flashes of orange.
        Each marker hovers,
                flicks past too
                        fast, we can't let it go we can't
                        see it or the next—

beyond our sphere, the expanse—
        white on white, the endless
                domes of our unknowing.
                Our knowing
                        what we cannot see

could very well whisk away
        our visible breath.

How the ones we loved
        well enough
                or not
                        would miss us with a white-hot
                        burning for as long as they

held on. And those who
        held old photographs
                would conjure our voices
                        above tree line, in whiteout,
                                the road drifted over.

Long after the photos
        have fallen, white
                flakes of ash
                        in a stranger's grate,
                                our distant, white-boned

daughter will warm her cold
        ear along the thigh of her lover.
                Her breath on his skin
                        white language
                                he can lose himself in

that white

    on white

        remake us

            windswept blue

                in its own image.

What is our place in the continuum? How do we find it? How much can we glean from those who have come before? March tells us that we have a place on this earth, but that our place is mutable. We have lives, and those lives are finite, even their span beyond our ken. March tells us that even though we can't know, we should pay attention.

Birds that have wintered over sleek down in March. No longer do camp robbers look scruffy and splay feathered or the ravens burly shouldered and rough mouthed. Instead, they're themselves, only streamlined, clean as washed cars (which won't show up here until after the geese). Chickadees, black capped and boreal, uncover more and more of the stashes of seed they cached all summer between scrolls of paper birch. Ravens play in updrafts by the steam plant all year, but in March they take their time rising and tumbling, throwing themselves extravagantly into blue sky. They fly some forty miles round-trip to reach favored nesting trees, but like to eat out at the Pizza Hut dumpster, and to entertain themselves in town.

For a few more weeks, bright-yellow plastic bags from the University of Alaska Fairbanks bookstore will hang out of dorm windows—minifreezers stocked with pints of Prudoe, sludge-thick chocolate from Hot Licks Home Made Ice Cream, or strips of smoked salmon or seal meat from home.

In March, a cow moose and two calves browse close to my house, gnash tips from whole stands of new willow until they look manicured, pruned. As the mercury heads up, people check the footlockers and plastic bins they've set outside as freezers all winter. I have to salvage the turkey in the snowbank on my deck, the last package of moose meat (a welcome gift from a hunter friend), and three unsmoked silvers from our trip to Valdez, where we limited out on fifteen-pounders, six each, in three hours. Three quarts of wild blueberries we'll stretch until July's abundance stains our lips and fingers. At the end of hard winter, we feast on stores laid by that won't abide full sun. When a visiting writer hits town in March, the potlucks turn profligate. Caribou stew, moose teriyaki, whole salmon fillets, Melissa's blueberry pie with the ceramic bird singing steam.

For a few more weeks, most bears in the Interior will stay holed up, cozy until the first grasses poke through patch snow, green blades they graze for breakfast, gaining energy to nose around for rodents and to gear up for caribou. Fly fishermen have tied whole swarms of flies from red-squirrel tail hairs and ptarmigan feathers. By March, they're itching to find a stream where their hooks won't bounce off ice. Not much longer. My friend who sleeps outside all summer prepares his couch under the eaves, and buys a length of new mosquito netting. Before long, the fastidious among us can wipe the winter's scrim from the outside of triple-paned windows, and open the whole house to air that won't bite. But not yet.

In March, men wield chain saws with four-foot bars to harvest blocks of ice eight-by-four-by-four from the gravel pit off Davis Road. World famous for its clarity and purity, Fairbanks ice draws carvers from around the world. In March, Ice Festival teams labor round the clock to carve an elaborate, ephemeral world. Ice carvers, performance artists every one. The Chinese team details ice-serpent dragons balanced on globes, right down to the scales and claws and flames of breath. Another team's entry careens—a stagecoach out of control, trailing six wide-eyed galloping horses, their manes flaring. The odd elegance of an eight-foot-high spike-heeled shoe set in a landscape where nobody sane wears such foolishness offers a study in juxtaposition. Kids, kept inside during deep cold, forced to bloom like hothouse flowers, festoon the ice castle playground, turrets, drawbridge, and dungeon. All day, they slide into the moats, and polish the back of the moat monster by riding him.

The ice carvers rough out forms with industrial blades set into handles as long as canoe paddles. Chisels and hammers reveal the nuances, and torches mend, seal, and polish. For fine details, the carver picks dental probes or heated wire. Many carvers make their own tools, just as Alaska Native carvers do, shaping handles for one palm, curved blades for the pressure of one set of muscles. At the airport I hear an impassioned French carver trying to make a dubious security checker comprehend why all the sharp edges in his carry-on could not possibly be considered weapons. "They create beauty only," he insists. The philistine makes him check his bag, and he frets all five hours to Seattle.

Why do grown people from all over the world devote a considerable part of their lives to creating art that will melt, evaporate, disappear into the air? Why do we love what is mortal?

Ice carving parallels good cooking or dance, intricate lifelong pursuits demanding attention and time, intended to be savored and shared, but over before you know it. For each maker, there's beauty in the made thing, but greater satisfaction in fleeting pleasure shared with others.

The concentration in the faces of some of the carvers makes me think of ancient masters, perfecting with great skill and care the briefest poems, then folding them into sharp-edged boats, and floating them down the river.

Our river, the Chena, flows into the Tanana, which continues into the Yukon before it empties into the Bering Sea. March is prime ticket-buying time for the Nenana Ice Classic, named for a small town at the confluence of the Tanana and Nenana Rivers. Each year a black-and-white four-legged frame, inexplicably called "the tripod," is positioned within view out on thick ice in the middle of the Tanana River. People place bets, day, hour, and minute, as to when the ice will shift enough to yank the rope and stop the clock attached to the other end on shore. The town of Nenana hires elders to watch, twenty-four hours a day, to make sure nobody tampers with the hardware, and to see if the ice is doing anything yet. People with a scientific bent have produced charts and graphs of depth of ice, ambient temperatures, water temperatures, rate of flow of the water underneath, wind chill, and snow cover. The people who guess by adding up their children's birthdays and subtracting their anniversary still win just about as often. The purse usually weighs in between two hundred thousand and three hundred thousand dollars, and the town welcomes the influx of ice watchers and ticket buyers, and depends on the much needed revenue.

Cash money out of ice—that's a lesson placer miners learned early in the twentieth century. Just after Felix Pedro struck gold north of Fox in 1902, prospectors rushed Alaska and filed claims all over the Interior. More than ten thousand miners came to try their hands, and before long the Old F. E. Company was serving meals to more than three thousand men a day at Chatanika. There's some debate, but legend has it that Pedro looked down from the hills and saw a steamship stranded on the banks of the Chena, and walked down to where E. T. Barnette, blustery mad, had been put ashore with the goods he had planned to use to set up a trading post much farther upriver. The stern-wheeler ran aground, and the captain refused to try to go farther. So Barnette set up shop, weighed Pedro's poke on scales later reputed to lean always toward Barnette's favor, and white people settled in.

Barnette supplied the miners, who used the winter to drag gear by dogsled up frozen streams. In summer they used flat-bottomed riverboats or heavily laden canoes to haul supplies. In March, though, with river ice not stable enough for travel, and the ground soon to be mired in the muck of breakup, the prospectors stayed put. Those who didn't have claims blessed with a constant source of water set about building glaciers, so they'd have a steady flow to send through the sluice boxes. They'd back up into the vee of a glacial valley carved out during the time of mammoths and mastodons. They'd sink two-foot stakes across the trickle of the stream easing out under the snowpack, and hang burlap in a knee-high wall. The burlap soon froze across, forming an ice dam. When it filled to the top edge of rough hopsack, the miners built another wall a few feet upstream, and continued the process all the way up the valley. The stacked ice melted gradually, washed over gold dust that settled along the low riffles of the sluice box, and carried away the lighter gravel and silt.

Some small operations still depend on the turnings of ice and sun. But the big guys just drill and blast and truck ore and crush it all year long, using cyanide leach heaps to coax the shiny stuff from the dross. In March, environmental engineers reintroduce the microorganisms that can metabolize cyanide. The substance deadly to humans nourishes certain bacteria, which thrive on turning poison benign. In the Interior, though, this bioremediation doesn't come cheap. The bacteria can't take Alaskan winters, so the miners have to start over each spring, trying to restore a balance they've upset, trying to solve a puzzle when they don't have all the pieces.

One day in March my first winter in Fairbanks I witnessed another puzzling spectacle—traffic. I hadn't seen four cars backed up since Seattle. I craned my neck to see what the holdup was. A couple of crews with wide scoops were busily shoveling snow *onto* the road. Cars and trucks honked, but the drivers were waving, not impatient.

And then I caught a glimpse of fur, the curl of tails waving above harnesses, a frosted parka with the ruff pulled tight. The Yukon Quest dogsled teams run the last leg of this thousand-mile race right into the middle of downtown. (The Quest runs Whitehorse to Fairbanks one year, Fairbanks to Whitehorse the next.) Trucks with dog boxes line Two Street, where fresh straw's laid out on the snow for the canine athletes, and hot drinks of various persuasions greet the mushers. Vets slip off the dogs' booties and check for ice between the pads of the paws. They take samples of blood and urine, and attend immediately to any dog brought in riding in a sled's basket.

Out at the Musher's Hall, future Quest racers line up—six-year-olds compete in one-dog sprints. Eight-year-olds can choose two or three. Usually the one pup pulling a scaled-down, hand-built sled quivers all over, barking and peeing, until the kid lifts her foot off the brake—a piece of plywood with metal zigzags nailed on to bite the snow. Green and eager, young kids and young dogs lean the sleds on one runner, then jolt wide-eyed back into the groove. The more savvy ones balance one foot on a runner, and cut their time by pushing with the other foot. Over a bonfire, organizers cook up dog food, a slurry of frozen chunks of dog salmon, vitamins, rice. At the trough, volunteers break the ice, and pour in hot water that steams for only a second or two.

Long after the party downtown winds up, sometimes days after the kid races at Musher's Hall, the last Quest finisher, bone-tired after more than two weeks on the trail, bumps into town. Die-hard race fans and race officials radio his progress, dogged and indomitable. Racers who grab headlines and cash get done in eleven or twelve days and take home endorsements. The last-place finisher gets a hot meal and the Red Lantern—proof that the musher and his dogs kept on, no matter what.

The no-matter-what can be considerable. One year a rare red aurora scared hell out of mushers who thought they were hallucinating. The year a bull moose stomped half of Susan Butcher's Iditarod team to death changed international safety rules—now all mushers pack guns. Meeting a winter bear, lean and hungry, isn't unheard of. Rookies who can't read river ice have fallen through, sled, dogs, and all. If they're lucky, another musher's not too many miles back. If they're lucky they make it to a trapper's cabin while they can still hang on to the sled, and they find dry tinder there. (Though my grandma'd say firmly, "If they were so lucky, they wouldn't have fallen through the ice.") Still, the Red Lantern's a testament to the human need to test our limits. And so we honor the final racer who staggers off the sled runners and tends to his team.

March's snow base, the foundation mushers prefer to fresh powder, the foundation skiers grip under the loose stuff, creates plain hard work for cabin dwellers and homeowners. Eventually, all the snow that's piled up since September has to melt, and you don't want to describe your home by saying a river runs through it. So, for all of us who haven't been diligent about keeping a swath cleared around our dwellings or building paths for runoff, March's fickle warmth demands action.

In the heaviest snow year in the last decade, 1992, a wet storm hit early, while the trees still held their leaves. Birches bent double, arching low over roads and trails, and zapping out power wherever they touched electrical lines. Abscission, the process that lets trees seal off leaves and conserve energy for the long winter, got interrupted. Some yellow patches held on to the white barks deep into the lightless season. This was costly for the trees, some of which remain stooped even now, years later. The snow kept on and kept on, and the cold turned fierce. Just filling a car's tank with gas became a shivering, chattering ordeal. From behind a wall of blowing snow, I heard a strange man's voice, "Oh well, at least we won't have mosquitoes the next week or two." Laughter got me home, where the roof groaned under the snow load. My friend Joe E. climbed up there and shoved whole snowbanks down, snow piling well past the rail on the back deck, snow up past the eaves in front. I tunneled from the driveway to where the front door should be. As winter wore on, I had to drag new snow uphill, up the path behind me, to keep the trail clear. The berms on both sides rose too far above my head for me to throw shovelfuls up and over. For three months I made shoveling my workout, my hobby, clearing the lost spout so the fuel man could deliver heating oil, keeping the path open so the Water Wagon guy could fill the holding tank.

Snow gains weight over the winter just like the rest of us. I cut shovel-sized blocks, strained to lift them over the deck rail, and pitched them downhill. Out front, it was just too much. I called a neighbor who has a backhoe. He got stuck and had to be winched free. An entrepreneur with a Bobcat offered to try. He didn't have the weight to keep traction. Finally, in March, I hired a commercial guy with a bulldozer—$450 to keep the basement wall from becoming a waterfall. Good deal. The snow mounds shoved up on each side of the house didn't disappear until July, growing shorter as the light grew longer.

Equinox, the day light and dark balance in duration, falls on or near my birthday, March 22. The wild extremes of midnight sun or dawn just before lunch and sunset just after fade for a moment. A weird relief—for a little while Fairbanksans won't meander slothlike through the dimness or bound exuberantly, wired on all that light. Instead, they have parties, large and small.

At Madge Clark's cabin, the beach party at winter solstice, complete with ice volleyball played by folks in long johns and jams, gives way at equinox to a huge bonfire burnt down to coals to roast salmon and halibut. Revelers quaff Russian vodka left from the last sister-city contingent from Yakutsk, vodka pulled from the snowbank, or sip tea steeped from rose hips dried over Madge's woodstove. The path to the outhouse gets tamped down well, and newcomers marvel at the accommodations—a Styrofoam seat for comfort, a stained-glass window for aesthetics. Sunshine streaming through color turns the head mystical. Off the eaves, the season's first icicles spike the light. Dancing and poetry and way too much food welcome spring's mucky promise to the Far North.

Over at the university, for four days in March, dance groups, artists, drummers, and families gather for the Festival of Native Arts. The potlatch honoring elders features jellied moose nose, raw turnips dipped in fermented seal oil, muktuk, Oreo cookies, Pilot bread, moose stew, caribou sausages, and Eskimo ice cream (a delicacy made of wild blueberries or salmonberries, snow, sugar, and Crisco). If we're lucky, somebody's relatives in Southeast Alaska got up in the night and spread hemlock branches just below the tide line. Herring roe clings to the bristles. We slip the twigs between our lips and use front teeth to strain the eggs from the piney needles. Icy and salty, each small orb gives up its life to nourish us.

For four days, drumming and dancing nourish us too. Some gestures recall old days, ancient ways to hunt, to laugh, to grieve, to live. New dances celebrate basketball, a mainstay in many villages, or commemorate an elder's first sighting of an airplane. Most Alaskan dance groups include everyone in the village who wants to dance or drum—old and young, little kids, teenagers, schoolteachers, health aides, elders. One year, though, a group came out made up entirely of old women. Their leader spoke into the microphone: "We know many kinds of dances, many kinds of songs. But tonight we will sing songs of love." And they did, haunting, mournful songs; teasing, playful songs; bold, unending songs; brief, longing songs.

At the time of contact, most Yup'ik villages used masks in their dances, masks carved into elegant plant faces or highly stylized into shapes of animal allies. Yup'ik carvers held great power, and produced physical evidence of the accepted awareness that people and salmon are one, carving features of both as one face. At the end of a mask's ceremonial life, it was returned to the tundra, to weather and to sink back into earth. Some early western collectors stole masks from their resting places. Others bartered for masks and regalia, but seldom asked about the items they saw as sources of profit. Museum collectors split up dance groups, not understanding their related functions, just seeing similar "specimens" as redundant. André Breton, the French surrealist, covered his office wall with the stunning juxtapositions of Yup'ik masks, and built on the earlier artists' visions. Most missionaries, though, saw only sacrilege, and banned the masks, the dances, the songs, the languages.

Cultural upheaval on this enormous scale has reduced the number of indigenous languages from forty-two at the time of contact to about six now spoken regularly (not just archived). All are one generation from fading. A university student describes her own household: "My mother speaks only Cup'ik, and doesn't write anything. I speak both Cup'ik and English, but I write better in English. My children speak mostly English, and don't always understand their grandmother." Whenever an elder dies, a whole library inside her is lost. Michael Krauss, a linguist with the Alaska Native Language Center, learned the Eyak language so he could do cultural and archival work with two elderly sisters, the last speakers of this tongue. The urgency of his task, gathering into dictionaries and archives the biomedical practices, the fishing and hunting traditions, the stories, songs, and personal anecdotes only these women could express, spurred him on. Then one sister passed away. I try to imagine the particular loneliness of being the only person alive who knows the jokes, the prayers, the warnings, the knowledge of an entire language. I try to imagine having only one person, not a childhood speaker, but a good scholar, to talk to.

Some villages have banded together to teach at home and in the classroom Yup'ik, Gwich'in, Tlingit, Inupiaq, Alutiiq. Young people have begun drumming and dancing, sometimes over the objections of elders who made the painful forced conversion to Christianity, and who have doubts about the old legacy. In March, Bethel hosts a huge dance festival. In Fairbanks, the Festival of Native Arts invites whole clans from Alaska, Canada, Russia. Some dancers wear button blankets and copper-inlaid headdresses. Some tie on heavily beaded mukluks and gesture rhythmically with dance fans made from the long white hairs that grow under a caribou's chin. Contemporary carvers adapt modern materials, such as brass bullet casings, into their work, just as earlier visionaries learned to use driftwood, metal tools, fish wheels. To pass along what is strong and healthy and nourishing from traditional ways was never more urgent. To adapt for one's own uses what is strong and healthy and nourishing in Western culture is quite literally a matter of survival. The difficult part comes in sorting out medicine from poison, a task done daily in every village, in every Native language.

I leave the dances late, and walk out under the gossamer canopy of the aurora, whistling to bring the lights nearer. For regular people, March nights, crisp and clear, offer the best chance to see the northern lights. Geophysicists, equipped with high-powered devices to measure, record, listen, transform into mathematics, and compare, prefer the infinite equations of deep winter. But in March, well past thirty, forty, fifty below, twelve hours of dark when you can stand to stay outside just work better. If the stars are out and the moon's not too bright, there's a good chance that the wispy high gauze of smoke isn't rising from a neighbor's chimney. In the growing dark, the scarf of light turns the diaphanous green of dragonfly wings, and begins to spiral. No one warned me that the lights can't sit still. Imagine the whole sky radiant with pink-tinged spikes rising in a disappearing arpeggio of light. Then the spirals uncurl, as if to reveal at their centers the essence of night. Literature and lore both teach that the void is eternal, the light ephemeral, except for those who embrace faith. But the cycles of moments, days, seasons, years, the cycles of solar flares and auroral magnetism teach that all permanence is illusion, that all life requires change and flux. I stand outside till my numb toes almost quit hurting. My reaction to ephemera, for the lights, for my life, is this—be here now. The river of light flash floods green horizon to horizon. My heart rafts that churning water.

Early morning—I wake to snow falling through still air. In March, great, nearly weightless flakes sift down over all creation. This new snow's so feathery and dry kids can't pack it into snowballs or forts. Any breath sends it swirling again. On this still morning, snow takes on the shape of black branches taking on snow. Laden birches sway, almost imperceptibly.

The sky's a kaleidoscope, white on white with a tinge of rose at the edges. A red squirrel's manic chitter chops air quick as a chef's knife. Then stillness. Eight miles out of town, up in the hills above the ice fog, I savor a luxury few people on the planet still have—quiet.

I do not hear my neighbors' quarrels or love moans, I don't suffer sirens or brakes or crashing metal all night. If a plane passes over, my husband can tell what kind it is, by listening, because it's the only one in our patch of sky. It works on a person, this quiet. It's not silence. No. The forest rustles quiet as pika in their tunnels, surfacing to check how much longer they'll have to stretch the store of grasses they harvested last season. The alder stand's hollows echo the tat-tat-tat reports of the resident pair of hairy woodpeckers, rebuilding their hidden nest.

The luxury of holding still long enough to take in these sounds works on a person. March snow offers the spirit a legacy of calm, if we give ourselves over to calm. Snow piles up in a deepening loneliness, if one's solitude suffocates. If a person has unfinished business with her conscience, now is the time to sort things through. For the industrious among us, snow's a chore cluttering front steps and the path to the outhouse. For a cross-country skier, ironing glide wax, corking kick wax, the new surface is a gift of access to backcountry. But for me, March snow brings home a desire to stay put. It's my job not to violate the unbroken surface around my house with footsteps or shovel, skis or sorrow. Just to watch, and to add my quietness to this day—that's ample, that's enough.

NO FOOLING—
APRIL IN TEXAS

NAOMI SHIHAB NYE

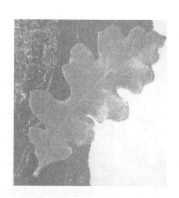

(APRIL 1ST) ILSE, OUR FAVORITE NEIGHBOR, AGE NINETY-EIGHT, can't believe I'm going to visit the governor today. She's sitting in her wheelchair in her tall green house in San Antonio's historic district, grinning at me. "What are you going to wear?" The TV burbles at low volume in the background. Ilse says, "I like him—he's cute. He has a good personality."

A small delegation of Arab Texans from all over our wide state have asked me to join them as some sort of chaperone, since I am the only one of us (how do they know this?) who has ever spoken with the governor before.

It is not what I would call a regular day.

What is a regular day?

Gov. George W. Bush welcomes us right on time. I have read that he receives 140,000 letters a year. It is amazing that he has a moment to do anything but read his mail. His assistant greets us in Arabic and tells us he used to work in the Middle East, which casts a warm glow into the formal room. Who can weigh the little things?

George W. believes in being a friend before you need something from somebody; don't just be a friend when you can get something back. I like him for his down-to-earth good spirits and his fluent, funny warmth. Every writer in Texas appreciates his wife, Laura, for having started the annual big-bash Texas Book Festival to benefit state libraries. Glossy literacy centers have been springing up on corners; funds are pumped into improved library collections across the state.

The general surge of "book interest" is something we can feel only grateful for.

So many people are already bugging the governor about running for president, but I wish he'd just stay here. We all sit in a circle. The governor seems to have an open heart. He listens well. He responds kindly to a Palestinian man's statement about his own family's losses and the ongoing inequity of American policy with Israel and Palestine. "Thank you," George W. says. "That was very well spoken. I appreciate your words." When a woman complains about the stereotyping of Arabs in Hollywood, he says, "Hollywood? Since when do we look to Hollywood for models? Hollywood tells my teenage daughters to have sex and take drugs!"

He is shocked when a Lebanese American engineer from Houston tells about being taken off an airplane, strip searched, and locked in a warehouse with someone who proceeds to mug him—for no reason beyond ethnicity. "Are you serious? This happened in TEXAS?" The governor jumps up and gets a phone number for a high official of the airlines. "Tell him I sent you."

The only thing he strongly disagrees with us about is the U.S. embargo on Iraq. He doesn't want to hear how disastrous this policy has been for the children and ordinary people of that country. Of course he wouldn't care for our opinion, since his own father enacted the embargo. "Why doesn't Saddam take care of his own people? It's not our responsibility."

How many of us feel we—and our children—deserve to be personally punished for Bill Clinton's immorality?

During our meeting, no one makes an April Fools' joke. I can't believe we miss the opportunity—especially since we're meeting with such a spontaneous person.

Chaperone? I'm the invisible spectator. Fly on the wall—what I always wanted to be. Soaking it in. I don't have to say much to feel I was really here.

I try to notice little things that Ilse might like to hear about. Cases of autographed baseballs along the governor's walls.

I drive home on the "back road"—Highway 281—hoping to avoid traffic and see more wildflowers. April, extravagant April, unfolds as the high point on the Texas calendar—the whole state bursts into bloom. Anyone who suggests that Texas really has "no seasons" is mistaken.

Occasionally, in winter, we have one freezing week. Every ten years or so, it's brutal enough to kill baby palm trees. We wear more sweaters than coats, it's true. We do have seventy-degree days frequently in January, and we never forget how lucky we are to have them. Autumn is characterized by frisky northers (big winds roaring south), and summer by our deeply contemplative, infamous heat.

During March, however, the wildflowers begin returning, bluebonnet patches in crevices by the roadside, so our eyes catch a sudden shimmering swath—we whisper gratefully, "They're back!" It's heartening to think of them sleeping under the dirt for so many months, then bursting forth again, right on time. By April the shining fields have reached what we call their exclamatory "peak." Even the most jaded residents may be moved to superlatives.

Indian blanket, cornflowers, clasping cone flowers, Mexican hats, Drummond phlox, toadflax—whole catalogs of exuberant names. Driving between solid banks of color feels rejuvenating. A visual boon, as if one's own spirit could rise up on a slim, clear stalk, pointing its hopeful face at the light.

I, for one, will never make fun of the "bluebonnet painters" in Texas. This much beauty is hard to reckon with in anything beyond sentimentally dazed terms.

And then there are cars.

An hour and a half between Austin and San Antonio once felt like a casual, comfortable drive. In Texas, where 752 miles separate Houston and El Paso, an hour and a half is, essentially, nothing. It's a single Lyle Lovett tape listened to twice. It's a good conversation, a relaxing reverie.

But this was before the onset of serious traffic, getting worse by the minute. Recently the famed AUSTIN CITY LIMITS feel excruciatingly far apart, and rush hour in that city now seems to be lasting all day long. (Once I read that you haven't really seen Houston traffic until you encounter a flaming mattress on the highway in hundred-degree heat. The next week it happened to me.) Somebody better get hopping soon on those light-rail bullet-train projects they keep mentioning, or our gooses are cooked.

Many of us remember when we had real fields between Austin and San Antonio . . . graceful farms, barns, and languid cattle have been replaced by enterprise, concrete, megastores, and factory-discount outlets that seem more expensive than regular stores. I remember hearing our former mayor Henry Cisneros say that someday the two cities of Austin and San Antonio would be joined together by a bustling corridor. The thought seemed revolting, but here it is, happening before our eyes.

Unfortunately, enough people have learned to take the "back road" — 290 West and 281 South — as an alternative route home, so a secondary traffic swarm is quickly developing. Only an hour after visiting the governor, I am driving west and south through gently rolling rural lands, casting my eyes into luminous fields of bluebonnets and Indian paintbrush. How thick they are, these Texas blues! How lush and fat the ground becomes, wherever they spring up! Blessings on Lady Bird Johnson and her highway-beautification projects of long-ago years! The seeds they cast continue to spread.

Recently I sat next to a man on a plane who deals in wildflowers, and he urged me to try planting some of my own again, though they're notoriously hard to get started in a yard. I ordered an expensive little sack from his company, and followed the demanding directions as carefully as I could. Pull out all weeds and grasses. Comb the dirt. Cast the seed loosely, shallowly. Keep it wet, wet, wet while germinating. Be vigilant.

This April our front yard explodes into blue, pink, yellow, and red in all its corners. I wish I had believed more in those seeds and planted them everywhere. Next year. The remaining seeds are stored in a tall jar with silica gel.

A few years ago, *Texas Monthly* magazine sponsored a writer to drive on every single stretch of roadway in this state and document his adventures. I can't even remember what his name was, but often, out in the countryside, I think of him, wondering . . . did he stop here? In Dripping Springs is a bakery called Wildflour — I whirl by, imagining all the delicious places we might pause . . .

Back home, I phone a photographer in the far west Texas town of Marathon and leave a drawled message on his machine. "Your dog is being held in the Alpine animal control facility. Please come fetch it immediately." I don't even think he owns a dog. But it is easy to picture the purple-and-blue Chisos Mountains off on his southern horizon and the way he might walk outside, stare at them, and shake his head.

I fax another neighbor and tell him our street is being renamed after him, signing the letter "Victor Flores, Division of Streets."

I go to see Ilse with oatmeal cookies after dinner. "The governor was cute," I tell her. "Very human, very funny. The flowers were great by the roadsides, and the traffic coming back was hell." She shakes her head.

Ilse's father owned the sixth car in the state of Texas. Somehow the idea of the sixth car is even more compelling than the idea of the first.

When our son heard this, he said, "Wow, the highways must really have been empty then!" and Ilse snorted like a horse. "Highways? Nothing was even paved!"

He was stunned. "What did it look like?"

"Very, very bumpy."

Our current mayor is proposing to change the pecan-shaded street perpendicular to our own, called Durango Boulevard, to Cesar Chavez, so he won't have to change a much more important street's name. Passionate placard-waving advocates demanding the important street have lately been pressuring city hall. Some of us love Cesar Chavez and his memory, but would prefer to honor him with a school, a park, or something new, so as not to lose "Durango," that lyrical word, or any other name that everybody is used to. Also, who wants to insult a great man's memory with a token gesture? Nuts, nuts, nuts.

What a peculiar concept—changing the name of a street. Consider all the people who found their ways home along sweet, stony Durango for the last hundred years! Names linger in the air, take on their own lives. The archives room at the library said "Durango" was one of a cluster of early streets named for Mexican towns—Saltillo, Tampico. A crumbling newspaper clipping said, "With names like this, those who were newly arrived from Mexico could feel easily at home."

I ask Ilse what she thinks about street names changing. She hates it just as much as I do. She dictates her own letter for me to fax to the mayor's office saying he is insulting our city and asking why he can't come up with something more creative as an honor for Chavez. He does not answer my fax, or hers. I can't imagine not answering someone ninety-eight years old. She was hesitant about including her age, saying, "He'll just pray I kick the bucket soon," but I did it anyway. I thought he should know.

Many people in the United States say they've "been to Texas" even if they've only driven across the spacious upper portion of the state. Ha. Undoubtedly they experienced mirages, saw their childhoods passing before them, imagined Georgia O'Keeffe materializing with a paintbrush in the upper-right-hand corner of the windshield, from her early Texas days teaching art in the canyon.

There is so much more to the story! A wide swoop of rich land to the south, replete with magical hills, cliffs, valleys, citrus groves, bird sanctuaries, coastal plains, hundreds of miles of dense piney forest in east Texas, a stunning far-western desert, the most breathtaking vistas and mountains anyone could ever imagine, and the most articulate sky. Yes, we have everything here. And we like it all.

I am very tired of people in other parts of the United States thinking that Texas has no trees. Geography lesson, please. They say to me, "Don't you miss trees, living in that desert?" and I must once again describe our semitropical wonderland, the ninety-eight-year-old pecan trees shading our house, the luxuriant mixture of plants and palms and vines and mesquites and live oaks in every direction.

San Antonio is the largest native pecan grove in the United States besides regions of Georgia. During autumn, one can barely walk down an inner-city sidewalk without crunching nuts underfoot. We are overwhelmed by nuts. We come home from a quick walk with stuffed pockets, even though our own yards are filled. The giant paper shells, the tiny, tight-skinned species...pecan-shelling companies in our neighborhood are nearly a hundred years old, going strong with their clattering cracking machines, beginning their whirrr in autumn and continuing...in April we still have gigantic sacks of uncracked nuts sitting in the corners of our kitchens.

We spend a great deal of time on the telephone trying to find tree trimmers who can "work us in" to their popular schedules. They're now charging four to five hundred dollars for trimming per tree. Unfortunately we have to spray for webworms, although we're very fearful of pesticides and their nasty residue. I interrogate the sprayer man, who has a wild-eyed grin and a jazzy hose. "Madam," he says, "you think I don't know my business?! Take it from me, I am the expert, you are safe, your nuts are safe, and I love what I dooooooooooooo!" He sings while he sprays. Maybe using pesticides is like sniffing glue.

I take Ilse spiced eggplant, yellow daisies. The Queen's Crown vines with their bursting pink bouquets are erupting on her wire fence again right outside. She rolls over to the door to look at them. Every day the air feels sweet and soft. I tell her about all the ducks on the river between our houses, how there seem to be more and more of them each evening. Long Vs of babies, new cousins landing from the sky... the purple martins have reestablished their chatty residence in their house on the tall pole. She wants to hear everything. Telling it makes me feel more alive. She is probably the most interested person I have ever known. Once she told me that a single daily newspaper had so much in it to think about, she didn't see how anyone could ever feel empty or bored.

Ilse has been crucially involved for decades in a great many conservation and preservation efforts affecting inner-city San Antonio. I always have trouble getting a grip on what her exact jobs or particular missions were, but that's only because she had so many. Her rooms are jumbled archives of news clips, ancient documents, theater ticket stubs, and vintage postcards.

She keeps her cards in photo albums, boxes, and drawers. She is always sending me off to find a card that she wants to show somebody, and she usually knows exactly where it is. "On that back shelf behind the Timmermann Sisters Cookbook in the little one-inch stack wrapped in rubber bands." Her Corpus Christi postcards are being displayed at the downtown library art gallery this month in glass cases. We had fun selecting them from her fabulous albums, moaning over all the exquisite vintage hotels that seaside city foolishly wrecked. Where were their preservationists? My great-uncle's antique white linens came out of our attic to be spread under Ilse's cards like creamy old-world butter.

Ilse wants me to tell her about all the lectures I'm going to.

Kathy Kelley, founder of Voices in the Wilderness, speaks against the sanctions in Iraq. She has traveled there nineteen times since the Gulf War, doing humanitarian work with mothers and children. She shows slides of skinny, dying children in Baghdad with exquisite faces that make us all cry. Arun Ghandi, grandson of Mohandas, speaks eloquently at an evening called Religious Organizing against the Death Penalty. When his grandfather was assassinated, he was only fourteen.

Sister Helen Prejean speaks incredibly well as part of the same program (she dives right into her gripping personal stories, instead of making introductory statements) as do family members of people on death row. Texas has the national reputation of being the state in the Union that sponsors more executions than any other, so the audience for this event is passionate and eclectic. I am a mixed bag of feelings on this issue and attend the evening only because my mother is in town and drags me there. She can't imagine a vegetarian being pro-death penalty—it's starting to seem strange to me too.

Dorothy Stafford, delightful wife of William, one of the most beloved American poets of the twentieth century, comes to visit. In her four Texas trips since Bill's death five years ago, she has developed an affection for our wildflowers, tiny cafes, and friendly people. She defends Texas now to people who insult it elsewhere. (Oregonians, for some reason, are particularly fond of insulting Texas. I asked some grumpy women in the Columbia Gorge once if they had ever been here, and they said, "No, but we're sure we won't like it." Then they paused. "Come to think of it," they said, "we *have* liked every Texan we've met.")

One year Dorothy visited us to get away from the rain, and it rained every day she was here.

This April we spend many happy hours just driving around out in the country, talking our heads off, on roads that never see too much traffic. We drive together up to the Willow City Loop Trail, which is not a city at all but a curling rural pavement an hour north winding among hills, cliffs, and trees, offering spectacular wildflower views. We take each other's photos in vast spreads of bluebonnets. Time with Dorothy always helps me breathe. Of course, we do all our happy meandering in—that culprit—the CAR.

This April we hold a tribute to William Stafford at the downtown San Antonio Public Library (which many people call the Red Enchilada due to its intense hue). Twenty writers from the region—San Antonio, San Marcos, Wimberly, Austin—read William Stafford's poems and talk about what he meant to their work and lives. Dorothy speaks generously about her life with Bill—we feel so lucky that she agreed to tell these heartening, beautiful stories.

On April 15, a stunning local legend of a friend, Pat Hammond, expert on kites and puns, hosts a tea party for Dorothy and makes each guest the most terrific party favor: a high-flying kite with a tail, folded out of tax forms.

Ilse Griffith turns ninety-nine on April 11, 1999.

When I forget the name of a book, Ilse remembers it. When I take her funny iced cookies decorated like ladybugs, she doesn't eat them, but keeps them around to look at. She marvels at them. Knowing someone her age who still marvels feels like an incredible boon. She saves a ladybug cookie for a little boy who is coming to visit soon. She says she often got in trouble as a child. For "talking too much."

Last summer, one of her legs had to be amputated from the knee down. Afterward at the hospital, her sunny personality startled me.

"I'm still the luckiest person in the neighborhood," she said.

"How so?"

"I don't have arthritis!"

She went back home to live by herself again. A neighbor named Bertha brings her food every day. I bring food whenever I have something worthy to offer. She always asks where I learned how to use so many spices. Our son, who does little chores for her such as vacuuming dust off her extremely high ceilings with a long nozzle, interviews her, making her speak into a highly sensitive microphone that she likes a lot.

She was present when ice cream first "arrived" in Texas, and her father, who ran a pharmacy as well as practiced medicine, had her sit on the porch with her sister to demonstrate "how to lick it."

Ilse insists there is nothing from the old days that she misses. "It's all still in here," she says, pointing to her lovely soft-haired head. She's a walking Texas archive, and we get to sit around with her every old day. I say, "Ilse, you are Texas, you know that?" and she hoots like a crane.

But later she asks me, "Say, why DO all these tourists still come to San Antonio? Everything good is gone." She keeps track of the news, grieving for violence, checking the weather.

On Easter Sunday she wears a gigantic bow in her hair, as if she has become a festive package. She asks my husband how anyone can call anyone else "civilized" when there is all this bombing and hideousness going on in Kosovo. I tell her I wrote some words exactly like that in my book for teenagers, and she asks me why I never gave it to her to read. I never even thought of it. It strikes me I've never hauled my guitar over to her house and sung her a song either. Why not? We just have too much to talk about.

Here we are, at the brink of a new millennium, dumb as ever... after all these historical wars, you'd think humans would have figured out something better to do. "Doesn't it amaze you," Ilse asks us, "that more people don't talk about history and how little we let it guide us?" Michael and Ilse discuss politics, whereas she and I talk only about little stuff and This Town. Whatever the topic, the neighborhood feels deep and rich when you walk in her door.

But then the ax falls.

I drop over to Ilse's in the evening with a fat slice of mushroom pie. Opening the door with my own key, I find a quietude looming that frightens me. Her little lamps are shining onto the smooth bedspread, but the chair where she usually sits is empty. The television is turned off. I shout her name, running through every room. I am so used to her cheery hello.

Then I race over to Bertha's house, and Bertha tells me Ilse fell in a doorway earlier that day trying to leave her wheelchair and walk on her prosthesis with a walker. "You know she is supposed to try to walk every day for exercise," Bertha says. "And a lot of times she doesn't do it. So I think she got weak."

Her hip is broken. "I tried to catch her," Bertha says, "but I am not that strong."

Where is Ilse now? The old Nix Hospital downtown, the hospital whose golden elevator doors are so exquisitely engraved you could weep for the lovely lost world every time you ride up in the elevator to visit somebody.

I race home and call the hospital room. Her voice is uncharacteristically tremulous. "I'm not very happy about this," she says. "In fact, I'm pretty blue. Why, why, why did I do something so stupid? Oh, I wish I could start today over again."

Tomorrow she will have hip surgery. They will give her a complete anesthesia. My mother and I visit her afterward—she is chipper and bright again, relieved to have woken from the surgery, laughing, telling us we're better than medicine, ordering all her meals for the coming week on a menu sheet—debating between pie and pudding—keeping us there much longer than we had planned to stay. "I turn ninety-nine," she reminds us, "on April 11, and I want to be out of here!"

That night she has a severe heart attack. The doctors call it her "second heart attack," saying she'd already had a mild one before we went to see her, which we did not know. All she mentioned to us was "some problems with her heart." She said she didn't ask what they were, and didn't really want to hear. "They moderated my medicine," she said, "and I'm better now."

After the second attack, she is given morphine that throws her into deep confusion. On her ninety-ninth birthday she cannot speak. Her grandchildren fly in from California and drive down from Austin. We stand in the hallway talking about traffic. When Ilse comes to, she is furious. "It's a dark day when I can't make it to my own birthday party!" she shouts. "I'm one hundred years old, and there's to be a large celebration tonight! Take me home! I don't want to be sick!" We tell her she is ninety-nine, not one hundred, and not to worry, there won't be any celebration until she's ready for it.

She keeps asking, "Am I dead?"

And then a parade goes by, banging and clanging, right under her window.

Try as I might, I can never get in the mood for Fiesta. Not when I was sixteen, recently moved to Texas, and stood puzzled with my mother in rare hundred-degree April heat to watch a spangled parade pass like a weird dream, and not when I'm forty-seven and live downtown right in the heart of it. Am I a misfit? Everyone else seems to love it. The newspaper is so excited. Everything relates to Fiesta. It's San Antonio's Mardi Gras. "Fiesta Fun Knows No Boundary" a headline reads. That is part of the problem.

There is the bombing in Kosovo on the front page, side by side with Fiesta. Bright flags go up on houses and telephone poles. Shiny streamers float from tree branches. The man pushing his EL PARAISO ice cream cart down the street clangs his bell with extra hope.

Public jubilation (for what? the end of our twelve-minute winter?), clamorous parades, shiny dresses, glittering floats, carnival rides—it all leaves me cold. At least people don't belt one another with flowers in front of the Alamo as they used to do. That's where the parade Battle of the Flowers came from, though nothing I read really explains it.

This year I feel slightly vindicated. Ilse confided to me recently that she doesn't like Fiesta either and hasn't for about sixty years. She says there are really two Fiestas, and she likes the secretive, quiet one (old ladies stuffing eggshells with confetti on the west side with Tejano accordion music playing on the radio), not the loud, social, public one.

Cartons, wrappers, straws, cold-drink cups, and dead balloons fill the streets. Our own historic neighborhood, called King William, hosts a one-day fair that started out as an intimate soiree years ago and has grown into a beer-swilling madhouse. Our neighbors sell parking spaces in their yards for five dollars a pop. Our son managed a roadside lemonade stand when he was younger. Even the open-air trolley would stop and let passengers leap out for a brisk lemonade.

A few months ago, *Journey* magazine, published by the AAA Corporation, invited me to write a Fiesta piece, and I told them they were knocking on the wrong door. After further discussion, they let me write a rather ironic "Letter to Fiesta" in which I describe Fiesta as a houseguest that keeps showing up when you're not ready to see him yet.

The truth is, I could never be ready for Fiesta. In my happiest moment I would not want to be drinking beer over at La Villita with my body pressed up against ten thousand other bodies. A newspaper writer asked a few years ago, "How did a medieval citywide beer bust ever become so popular?"

Nor would I wish to watch another parade float go by for the rest of my days. Not a River Parade, nor a Night Parade. How long does it take to fold a paper flower? The floats are made of millions of them. I describe my problem with Fiesta as being partly mathematical. Once I heard it takes seamstresses an entire year to sew a single sequinned dress for a duchess. There's a Coronation Ball and a King and a Rey

Feo, Ugly King, only slightly more interesting. Some people grow up dreaming of this stuff. Frivolous? Make your own conclusions.

Fiesta makes me crouch in a dim room, muttering.

And this year, perched in Ilse's high hospital room over Navarro Street, it seems stranger than ever.

Taking a walk on the day before Fiesta officially began, I breathed in the cool morning air, ripe and rich with jasmine and honeysuckle scent from all directions. Now this was worth doing. No one was downtown yet, except the regular old people who live and work down here. It felt like an edge, a quiet space. Nobody was making any money yet. No neon necklaces, no trash. People tinkered in their yards along King William Street, trimming flower beds, sprinkling curly vines, preparing for the hordes and masses of Fun Folk. Maybe I don't have a Fun Gene.

Your Name Engraved on a Grain of Rice

Blazing pink shirts spill into streets, garden green, full-throated
fluorescent, fiesta red. Humdrum the dim subtleties! The mothers haul

parasols for sun toward Ferris wheels which may or may not have that
    last pin properly placed. Who cares, these days? You could die just
    eating.

They drag small stools for sitting at parades and toddling boys who kick
the giant Coke cups pitched onto curbs, toeing the sweet and sticky
    trails.

Thirsty places inside their mouths grow and grow. Soon they too would
    spend
extra for what they usually pour from the big bottle in front of TV.

City Hall shrinks in a cluttered grid of Tilt-a-Whirls and Rocket Rides.
Now our local headliners may watch their constituents flip upside down

for fun. How much have they done to lose our faith? See them reach
    their
people here, propellers of hair spinning out. See the people thread

the crowd to smash a bottle with a ball. All they need
is a break in schedule to sizzle again. Give them kings, confetti,

cascarone eggs cracked over their heads. Dribble of itchy bits down the
 back
of the shirt, who cares, insurance, who cares, brown spots on the back
 of the

hand? In this land of glistening ballgowns and floats of flashing girls,
everything shifts. Even if her waving hand is gone

in two minutes. They trade in lonely houses for the crowd,
beer-scented blaring, bras without shirts,

the sloping, sweltering flesh. They mesh. They lose their quarters. They
guffaw. They ought to do what that booth says, put their name on the
 littlest

grain of rice like magic, but what about Fernando, Dagoberto,
Henrietta, Marielena? Aren't they too long? What about Octavio

Hernandez-Salvatierra and his 20 uncles and their 77 hopes? What
 about
the year we planned to trick everything gloomy like a bad yard

with sudden roses turning nice or something that swells and stays
 swelled,
bubbling and softening, changing its life?

—from Fuel, BOA Editions, Ltd.

Ilse moans, "I wish I could change what happened. I wish I never
got out of my wheelchair to try to walk that day…dumb, dumb! I
just keep feeling mad at myself." We all tell her it is not her fault.
Cymbals in the streets. The tinkle of the Ferris wheel over at the carnival a few blocks away…

Some days, depending on how much painkiller they've given her,
she is thrashing and disturbed. Other days she's clear as April air. "I
love you so much," I tell her, on one of those good days. She squeezes
my hand. "Well, I love you! I love everybody!" The nurses confer
with me out in the hall. "Who is this amazing woman?"

We've just had a happy visit discussing the recent exciting purchase
of the long-neglected Hot Wells property, a mysterious, fabulous spa
on the south side of San Antonio that Ilse remembers from her childhood. The tangled property has been sitting, gloomily abandoned,

for years. Will they bring it back to life? Will something wonderful be resurrected? Blaring trumpets under her high window! Banging drums! She says, "Is this the thirty-fourth parade of the week or the thirty-fifth?"

Then she grips my hand. "Will you keep on loving me even if I turn into a very bad girl?" she asks.

"Go ahead! Do it! It's spring, let's all be bad! Spring fever! But what can we do?"

Later that day I walk along the San Antonio River with my niece Caroline and a group of kids from her Catholic school class in Corpus Christi. They've been on a class retreat up in the hill country west of here. They prepared their own meals from menus they planned themselves, hiked, boated, and performed skits by an evening bonfire. Now they want to write poems for a couple of hours. It feels very redemptive to be with kids after being in a hospital so many hours.

I make them look at baby ducks and the graceful green iron footbridge and the backs of lovely houses and flowers in giant clay pots. We try to notice the smallest things we can: ants, crickets, lizards, the soft brushy nub on a long stalk of grass. We sit on stairs next to the River Authority building and write together. What unwinding lines the birds reel out, spirals and trills . . . a crane rises up from the reeds. Breeze fills us. The kids are bubbling over with poems and want to read what they write again and again and again. They say, "It's so cool down here! We never knew San Antonio had such great secret places!"

Later, one of the mother-chaperones writes me a nice note: "It was so refreshing for me to stop all my mind's work and just listen . . . to the wind, the vines, the water. It's a life lesson I hope to remind myself of often."

Me too. Especially when there are all these other things: How could the shooting disaster at Columbine High School in Colorado happen during National Poetry Month (also National Welding Month) at a school named for a wildflower?

How could it happen at all?

A confusing marquee appears on the Selena store on Broadway. Selena, the incredibly talented and popular Latina singer, was murdered here in Texas a few years ago by the so-called ex-president of her fan club. Her store, still existing right near our old Brackenridge

Park, features high-voltage, pepped-up fashions under a sign simulating her own signature. The marquee changes week to week. Now it's:

LOOK LIKE A BOMB
WHEN YOU GO TO THE PROM

Are we losing our minds?

Our neighbor Penny and I sit on either side of Ilse's bed, holding her hands. Her arms are darkly bruised from all the injections and IVs. Ilse's shouting, "Nein! Nein! Nein!" at regular intervals. She's staring at something we can't see past the ceiling. The nurses ask, "Does the number nine have any special meaning for her?" and it hits me. German was her first language. I whisper into her ear, "I don't think they understand German here," and she switches channels immediately to "No! No! No!"

I say, "Ilse, I wish I remembered more from my German classes" and recite a few lines of a poem in German, about smoke rising over the chimneys and drifting here and there, and she grows calm. Her granddaughter comes to be with her in the afternoon, and to spend the night.

More than any of the rest of us, Ilse wanted to see that year with the three zeroes lined up. She dies on April 28 at seven in the morning. The key to her house is lying on my desk.

Walking around the neighborhood that evening after dinner, crossing the bridge from our side of the river to Ilse's, passing through the jasmine tunnel, gulping great sweet breaths of scent, we think: this is the first dusk in ninety-nine years that Ilse did not see. Our hearts are sinking in the darkness. We can barely speak to one another.

The neighborhood feels too quiet. Adrift. Lonesome for its queen.

Marla Akin, friend and postcard collector who loved Ilse too, sends an e-mail from Austin: "I feel as if some great ship has gone down, loaded with gold coins—Ilse and her memories and her stories. I keep picturing an especially lovely hand-tinted card of a lost ocean liner."

We need to get away. So we pack a few blue jeans and blue-jean jackets, our tent, some books and notebooks. We drive west on I-90. It's a family ritual. We buy cheese pockets at Haby's Alsatian Bakery in

Castroville. We eat enchiladas in Del Rio. We keep track of the latest Spurs basketball scores on the radio.

The Pecos River Gorge stuns us once again with its sudden beauty. A reputation for bigness is one thing. Brash bravado, cowpunchers with swaggering strides, macho manners, bold bigness jokes—not very appetizing, any of them.

But that's not what I think of when I think of Texas.

Not at all.

Having lived here thirty years, I can vouch the word is "space" and its derivatives: spacious, spaciously, spaciousness.

Commodious, capacious, ample, roomy, expansive.

Forget all those cars stacked up on the freeways in urban areas. Look beyond them.

Horizons, the vast tablets of days, the moving texture of sky. We have wide margins. Face it. A person who lives with wide margins becomes a different person. What does it do to the mind? The mind expands.

In April, the fragrant delicacy that permeates the broad atmosphere and air of this shimmering state only sweetens the page.

We drive around the abandoned buildings of Langtry—no one has purchased "The Sample Cafe" yet. I still have Helen Sample's name taped to my file cabinet. Someone at the icehouse in Langtry told me I might be able to buy it from her, cheap, but she lives in Laredo, and what would I do with it? In Dryden, an astonishingly dried-up west Texas town, the single shopkeeper still remaining sits at his front window staring out. Used to be five hundred people here. Now there are five. Used to be the train stopped. Used to be sheep.

Even he doesn't really live here. He lives in Sanderson, the next town, and commutes. We've paused at his enterprise next to the post office for a root beer and a toothbrush, on the way to Big Bend National Park for a couple of nights' camping . . . our favorite place on earth.

"Do you like Big Bend?" we ask him.

"Never been there," he drawls. "Lived around here all my life and never been there."

How is this possible? It's only a few hours west and south. He has a truck out front, a jaunty tip to his cowboy hat, and an enthusiastic grin.

He shrugs. "Well, I turned left off Highway 90 to go there once with my wife, and some huge thunderheads rolled up, you know those really big, dark ones, and I was looking out at all that sky and those mountains and nothing in between us but desert, and I thought, do I want to be out here in the wild if a giant storm rolls in? I thought, no, I do not. And I turned my car right around."

RACING IN PLACE

33 HOOSIER HAIKU

MICHAEL MARTONE

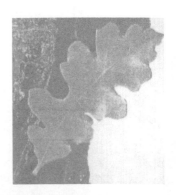

1

The first thing you did was tune in the radios. Everyone had the new transistor radios, most the size of cigarette packs, in pastel hard-shell plastic. Some were upholstered with protective leatherlike vinyl with flaps and snaps and die-cut openings for the gold-embossed tuning dials, a slit for the coin-edge volume wheel, an aperture for the ear jack out of which an always too short and easily kinked wire attached to a single waxy plug you screwed into your head. But today, race day, no one listens to the 500 on the earphone. My father and the other fathers in the neighborhood are pouring a patio. It's what they do on Memorial Day.

2

The elms, for some reason, haven't died on Parnell Avenue, and their vaulting branches arch over the street, throwing it into deep shade. The parade route runs from State Boulevard along Parnell out to the War Memorial Coliseum. We like to sit near the Dairy Queen, unfolding our lawn chairs in the parking lot driveway. We have brought the big radio with the stitched handle. It is the size of my school lunch box. The cars at the track make a swishing sound as they zoom about. I sit on the curb and think I see the horses' hooves throwing sparks. A semitrailer is hauling a retired F-86 from the air base out to be displayed on the coliseum's lawn. The Navy Club's bus-long gray destroyer, number 48, floats by above me, its wheels hidden by a skirt of waves.

3

My mother and the other mothers are sitting on the patio next door, a concrete slab in the middle of the yard. It is cured to a marble white. The furniture is new, webbed candy-colored nylon and aluminum tubing. The Thompsons' patio. It was poured last year. The men are wearing white T-shirts, khaki pants, and their old work shoes, standing in a circle around the wheelbarrow filled with crushed ice and bottles of Old Crown beer, tuning in, each one holding his little radio next to his ear, worrying the tuning dial, thumbing up the volume. One by one they find WOWO, the local station on the network, coax the static into sound, cocking the radios at angles to align their tiny antennae. It is primitive. It is magic. It is like they are blowing on a smoldering tinder to get it to spark. And they do.

4

The thrum of the engines brought us outside. We looked up, shading our eyes against the sun. The blimp was just above the tops of the dying elm trees and descending, it seemed, toward the field behind our house. Then there was a change in the engines' pitch, and the blimp yawed and floated up and away. We ran to the car to follow, slowly cruising through the meandering neighborhood streets. Stretched out on the backseat of the '57 Chevy, I looked up at the blimp as it wallowed overhead, framed first in the back window, then in the one at my feet, then in the one above my head as it maneuvered, and my father, turning, came about and circled beneath it. It settled, at last, in a field near the three rivers, a ground crew hauling it down. The cars that had been chasing it parked in a big ring around it. It was May, and the blimp was on its way to take up station above Indianapolis. Moored, it levitated a few feet off the ground. We all sat transfixed on the car's hood and watched the blimp float but stay perfectly still.

5

Another radio joins the nest of transistor radios on the grass nearby, amplifying the tinny voice of Sid Collins, the Voice of the Indianapolis 500. The men begin to work, finishing the frame and leveling the bed while others mix the cement and sand. I hear beneath the Voice in the grass a sound like static, but it isn't static. It is the pulsing siren of the racers' engines flying around the track, the two-beat peal as they scream past the mike, an *E* then a long *m*. EEmmmmm. But so small, an insect humming in the greening grass. There will be locusts this summer idling in the trees. Summer is racing toward us. I coast my bike down the Kaimeiers' drive, join the other kids on their bikes doing laps around the manhole covers on either end of the street.

6

I go to college in Indianapolis. My mother went to the same school. Near noon, I cross the muddy campus. I slog along on the way to class. The bells ring out, as they do every hour, every day, the opening bars of "Back Home Again in Indiana." It is a gray day with the clouds lowering. It is often gray, the result of the atmospheric accident in which we live. Ground zero for an occluded ceiling generated by the lakes, the wind, the flat, flat ground. Back home again in Indiana, I whisper, where the sun refuses to shine. Then in the silence after the tolling, I hear a distant screech, a prehistoric trumpet, a beast's yawning scream originating high up in cavities of a skull. The scraps of sound drift in the thick air. Tire tests at the track across town.

7

The race is on on the kitchen radio. I sit at the kitchen table coloring in the outlines of race cars. My mother has drawn a simple template — a side view of two wheels, the tube of the fuselage, a wedge of windshield, a hump of the rear engine. I have traced out thirty-three copies, placing a clean sheet of paper on top of her drawing and following the outline. Now I am coloring each a different color. On the radio there are announcers in each turn of the track and on the straightaways. They follow the leader around the lap. Sid Collins, the Voice of the Indianapolis 500, says that this is the greatest spectacle in racing. But I've never seen it. It is only on the radio. The table is layered with the brightly colored cars, scrambled together, a wreck of color. I stay inside the lines I've outlined in black. I know that the shades of green are unlucky. The blues are beautiful and limitless. Outside my father is mowing the lawn. I hear the mower's engine fade as he goes around the far side of the house.

8

There are high school bands, but they are mostly quiet, saving their practiced marches for the reviewing stands on the other side of the river. The drummers thump a cadence of the wood sticks against the metal rims of their drums. They slide their feet on each step. I see green puttees and canvas gaiters of the Legion and the VFW posts' colors. It is strangely quiet for a parade. The swish of cloth. The silky flags sliding along the polished poles. The whispered humf, humf of a drill sergeant. Each unit slowly disappears down the dappled tunnel of the street. The driveshaft turns beneath the flatbed truck, an honor guard, at parade rest around a mock-up of a tomb on the carpeted bed. In the silence, the echoes of hundreds of portable radios. The race in Indianapolis, a hollow drone.

9

My father drilled a hole in a rubber-coated baseball, threaded a rope through it, and knotted the end so it wouldn't slip back through. On the other end of the rope was a handle. In the field behind the house, he twirled the ball around above his head. I stood to one side with a bat and tried to hit it as he banked it toward me. It zoomed by. I was getting my timing back for summer, he said. A garbage can lid was on the ground, a makeshift home plate. The ball wobbled, warbled a hiss as it made its orbit. Around and around. I'd catch it coming in the corner of my eye and step into the approaching sound.

10

The simulators were painted gunmetal and arranged three to the row before the movie screen. I was driving through a neighborhood like mine, though its colors were faded or too brightly lit. There were people walking on the sidewalks wearing clothes from when I was a kid. The women wore white gloves and hats with net veils, the men wore suits and ties. A freckled boy, his head shaved, broke away from his parents and darted out into the street lined with old elms. I seemed to slow to a stop. The machine in the back whirred and clicked, recording whether my brake pedal was depressed. Then I was entering a highway, a new interstate, its concrete brilliant white. All the turn indicators were ticking in the room. Then it was raining and it was night. I'd glance at the speedometer from time to time as I was instructed. The needle slowly swept around from zero as I sped up. The room filled with a throaty engine noise. The soundtrack ran through the gearbox. The brakes complained slightly as I pulled into the driveway of a house like my house. The machine in the back came on again to see if I had put the car in park and turned the key to stop the engine. I had put the car in park. I had turned the key. I waited a few more minutes, my seat belt buckled, until the bell rang for the next class.

11

I remember the smell of the newspaper, the way it was folded to the page with the starting grid, the ten rows of three cars each, the blocks of information—number, driver, owner, sponsor, engine, body, speed. My father's scribbled notes as each car dropped out of the race. Engine. Transmission. Tires. Crash. My mother, finishing up the dishes, picked up the coffee cup my father had forgotten he used to weigh the edges of the paper down. There was a blot staining the top of the statistics, a blurred circle, smeared, smearing. My father sat and listened to the race's murmur, my baseball mitt on one hand, the other hand rubbing the neat's-foot oil into the darkening pocket.

12

The pace car moved by at the walking pace of the parade. We were on the Parnell bridge over the St. Joe. Ricky Brown was going on about the 'Vette, the particulars of its engine displacement, the block's bore, the compression ratio. A girl from our high school was a queen of something that year, and she waved at us. Too cool, all of us but Ricky turned away from the parade and, leaning on the bridge's railing, looked at the river just below the deck, swollen and running fast in spring. Ricky called out to the guy driving the car, hunched over listening to the radio, "Who's leading? What lap?"

1 3

A Saturday before the race, I went with my dad to May Sand and
Stone to pick up the bags of cement and sand. He had an Olds Cut-
lass coupe, white with a blue top and bucket seats. In high school I
would total it, running off the road into the ditch. The windows were
cranked down, and the radio was cranked up high to the time trials.
We followed the trace out to the gravel pit. I liked hearing about the
driver on the bubble, the slowest car about to be bumped by another
qualifier. The overgrown ditch on the side of the road was all that
was left of the canal built to connect the Great Lakes with the Mississippi, bankrupting Indiana before the Civil War. The water was stag-
nant and weedy. On the bobbing cattails, red-wing blackbirds perched.
Their calls were like the rattles of mixing balls in cans of spray paint.

1 4

Small planes circled, dots followed by a dash of their banners, their
advertisements unreadable from this distance, traced their spiraling
paths. I was driving home, north, to Fort Wayne. I took the wrong
exit on purpose to circle the city the long way around so I could listen to the race. The radio said the race was halfway through and under
a yellow caution flag. A survivor of the most recent wreck was thank-
ing God. Thirty-three miles of four-lane beltway until I-69. I worked
my way between the other cars and trucks, racing. I could not see
the track from the highway, just the planes trailing their exhaust of
messages, circling above it in the distance.

1 5

The race, on the radio, is background, drowned out by the stutter of
the electric clippers my father uses to sculpt the edge in the backyard.
His shirt is off, stuffed into his back pocket. It looks like a tail. Mother
sits on the chaise lounge on our slab of a patio, painting her toenails
a bright red. Two orange extension cords snake out through the grass,
one winding toward the radio and one attaching to the clippers. We've
planted impatiens in the shade of the garage; the egg-carton nursery
flats nest inside each other. I coil the hose next to the spigot. Maybe
later we will wash the car.

MICHAEL MARTONE

16

I walked to my high school. I took State Boulevard, which was an old township road running east and west that had, when the city grew up around it, become a main crosstown corridor. When I walked it, during the rush hours, I kept pace with the cars crawling along in the daily traffic jams. Sometimes a string of cars would break away only to stall again at the next light, a half block ahead, where I would catch up again. Ahead of me was my high school, North Side, across the St. Joseph River from the Old Crown Brewery. It was spring. The brewery made the neighborhood reek of fermented spent grain. Behind me was North Highlands where I lived and where, as it was high ground, the radio and television stations planted their transmission towers. Coming home, I saw the strobing beacons on each become visible as the sun set and the city grew dark. The cars creeping along next to me in the street had their windows down. It was spring. The patter of the radio leaked out. A song, a weather report, the ninth caller. As I walked along, the volume seemed to fade and pulse with the strips of tiny suspended warning lights at the other end of the road.

17

A sign says this is the deepest hole in Indiana. Empty yellow dump trucks follow the access road cut into ledges screwing down to the quarry's floor where groaning excavators gnaw at a trench. I am in a metal observation cage extending out over the lip of the pit looking down forever. The loaded trucks spiral up, trudging around ever widening loops scored against the sloping walls to the top. The reports from the track of the time trials and practice laps are running on the P.A. system, interrupted by an announcement that someone's order has been filled or someone else has a phone call. Dust steams up to the brim. I am floating above the dust swirling below me, looking at it roil through the open steel grid at my feet. Suddenly, Phantoms from Baer Field rip by overhead, practicing the Memorial Day flyby.

18

"Stay tuned to the greatest spectacle in racing," the voice on the radios said. The transistor radios seemed to be fading, their batteries taxed.

The cement of the patio was setting up. In a corner of the slab, our fathers allowed us to write our names with a ten-penny nail and to press our handprints into the spongy surface. We washed our hands at the spigot, a puddle of mud forming at our feet. We stretched out on the grass. A tire commercial. A milk commercial. An interview in the pits. The cars roaring by drowned out the people speaking. I tried to hold the level level. I held it above me, up to the sky, nudging the bubble back and forth between the hairlines in its little yellow tube of fluid.

19

My mother went to the race once. When she was in college in Indianapolis, women from her sorority rode in the festival parade before the start in vintage cars around the track. My mother rode in a horseless carriage made by Studebaker. She wore an antique duster and a big hat with goggles. She waved to all the people in the grandstands, a half-million people. The speedway becomes the second-largest city in Indiana on the day of the race, she always says. Making deviled eggs on Memorial Day, flicking the dollop of yolk mixed with mayonnaise in the cup of the hollowed-out half, dusting the two dozen halves with paprika and pepper, she remembers the boxed lunch she ate that day in the sunny stands, the race itself an intermittent distraction in the background.

20

When I was in kindergarten, I was in the parade. I rode a float, sitting in a lawn glider that glided back and forth beneath an arching garden arbor decorated with paper roses and on a lawn of artificial grass staked with lawn flamingos and a plastic birdbath with real water that got us wet when the wind blew. The trailer was pulled by a white Impala, and my father was in the backseat looking out the back window up at me riding on the glider. I wore a crown I kept for years afterward on the globe in my room. I remember the old trees making a roof over us, how slow we went down Parnell, the way people on each side of the street waved with one hand while the other hand held a radio to an ear.

The high school loop ran north and south from one Azar's Big Boy to the other through the center of town. The lights were timed, and we hit every one, not stopping. We went over rivers and under overpasses where sometimes hulking Nickel Plate or Wabash trains clanked on tracks above us. The streets were the old state highways, wide and one-way, lined with glass globed lights still painted on the top to black them out from the air. You couldn't be too careful. We talked, my buddies and me, about going to Ohio where they sold 3.2 beer to minors, but we never did. We were unable to escape the gravitational pull of the place. Our high school going by. The musk of the brewery and the slow-moving river choked with cottonwood. WOWO on the radio. "I have no desire to ever see that race. You sit in one place and see the cars for, what? A second or so and then wait a couple of minutes for it to happen again." There, the neon cross of Calvary Temple. There, the old City Light powerhouse. There, the armory. Powers Hamburgers. The Lincoln Tower. The Old Fort, a replica of the old fort, a guard walking the walls looking out for the vandals we fancied ourselves to be.

I have a picture of my mother and father sitting on their graves. Always planning ahead, they purchased the plots in the Catholic Cemetery years ago. They bought the monuments too, already engraved with their names and birth dates. They were optimistic enough not to have the nineteen of the death date inscribed, but their names are there and their birth dates. The markers are simple slabs of polished granite the size and shape of swing-set seats, very low to the ground. It looks as if they are sitting on the ground. They are smiling. We went there one Memorial Day to look at all the graves. My father's parents' and sister's, my mother's parents' and grandparents'. We ended up checking out how their own graves were doing. There they were. The stones were supposed to be that small and low to make the maintenance of the cemetery efficient. No flowers allowed. There were flags on Memorial Day, but those were taken back up after a day or two. In the future, the mowers would cut right over the stones as they sank the rest of the way into the ground.

23

Our bicycles are piled in a wreck we have simulated. We are sprawled, casualties, on the strip of grass between the curb and sidewalk. After a while, we forget we have died. We look up at the streamlined and spoiled clouds, racing.

24

My father went to the time trials one year, but it rained. The showers were scattered, and when the sun came out they tried to dry the track by driving ordinary cars and trucks around it. He sat in the fourth turn and watched fire engines, ambulances, wreckers, buses, and pace cars speed by, accelerating the evaporation. Just as it was drying off, race cars with their big slick tires revving their engines in the pit lane, it rained again. Bored, ushers with opened black umbrellas walked around the two-and-a-half-mile oval, and in the homestretch a few of them broke away from the group with longer and longer strides, trying to be the first to cross the finish line.

25

Behind the chain-link fence, the patients of the State Hospital and Training Center watch the parade. Some of them march along behind the fence, falling into step with the passing bands and color guards or drifting along with the creeping floats. The fence runs for what would be five blocks along Parnell. The streets that dead-end at the boundary of the hospital grounds are used as staging areas for the parade's start. The patients wear hospital gowns and robes of pastel pinks, blues, greens, and yellows. They press their faces into the fence. Some climb a foot or two to get a better view, their fingers wrapped in the weave of the metal links, until the orderlies, who have been listening to the race huddled around the radio in an old ambulance, peel them off and plop them on the ground again. The ones who have been shadowing the parade are stopped when the fence turns a corner blocks away. They race back to the beginning, focus on a new drum major who trills his whistle, high stepping in place. The patients turn with him and begin to march once again.

26

Stuck in the stalled traffic on State, this year's pace car, a red Ford
Mustang. The local dealerships of the winning manufacturer would
get a shipment of special-edition models each year to show off. You
would see them racing around town, advertising the brand's fortune.
On each door was a decal of a wheel with wings and the array of all
the racing flags. One day each year, pace cars appeared, migratory birds
or butterflies. A woman sat at the wheel blowing bubbles of bubble
gum. Spring.

27

One year, something happened. A wreck at the start of the race had
killed several drivers. I remember listening to the restart in school a
day later. I was in art class rolling out clay to coil into pots. Others
were kneading the clay or cutting blocks of it with wire. The teacher
was firing pieces in the small kiln, and you could hear the whoosh of
air as it burned. The announcers at the track were subdued and sad.
It seemed the completion of the race was more of a chore now, something that had to be done. The engines sounded muffled. I liked my
art class. It was quiet as we worked. The teacher moved from table to
table, here smoothing the lip of a pitcher with his thumb, there ap-
plying a slip with an old brush. The radio muttered in the corner.

28

Sid Collins, the Voice of the Indianapolis 500, will kill himself. I'll
hear the news on a radio in a car in Indiana.

29

We sit on the car hood at the end of the runway. The Phantoms, in
formations of two, glide over us, their flaps flared and gear down. In
the distance, we see them touch down. Then the afterburners ignite,
and they leap back up off the shimmering runway. The pilots are logging hours on the weekend. Above us, pairs of jets bank and turn,
circling on approach. Climbing, their engines make a sound like

ripping blue cloth. Some cars in the race this year have turbine engines. They whine and whistle on the radio, breaking records during practice laps. There's a war. There is always a war. But it is far away.

3 0

I practice driving in the cemetery. My father sits in the passenger seat playing with the radio. The yellow Rambler is a company car he bought at auction, a decal of the company's logo peeled from the door. It's a big cemetery. In the older part there are old trees, and the monuments are columns and urns and obelisks. Wrought-iron fences or low walls of stone outline family plots. The roads curve around in circles. I stop and start and signal. I ease out the clutch, and the engine bucks. I can gain a little speed on the straightaways of the new section where the markers are in ordered rows and next to the ground. Mary, the Mother of God, directs traffic at an intersection. I go by my grandmother's grave again. A troop of Boy Scouts carrying backpacks filled with toy flags sifts between the stones, dipping down to the ground, in ones and twos, to decorate them for the weekend.

3 1

I walk the sidewalks of the old neighborhood. Summer started after Memorial Day, and I spent those summers riding my bike behind the city crews cutting down the dying trees. The chipper with its long-necked Victrola hood sounded, as it bit into branches, like the whooping engines at Indy howling out of the corners. The people who live here now are not home. At the parade perhaps. Picnicking. At the cemeteries. In cars. At the race. Or on their way someplace listening to the race on the radio. The patio is still here. The owners just hosed it down, and it is drying in the light breeze and warming sun. My name and the names of my friends. And, there, the dimple of my handprint holding a puddle of water in the depression of the palm. In some other backyard I hear the chirp of a radio.

3 2

We dream about the moonlight on the Wabash. We sang it before our own bike races along the meandering side streets and oxbow loops of the neighborhood. We sang the song like we heard Jim Nabors sing it on the radio before the race. We tried to swallow the words as we sang them, holding notes on the verge of a yawn. We sounded, to our own ears, operatic and old-fashioned and grown-up. We marveled at the transformation of his voice every time he sang. Our own voices were changing. Things could change. The crowd cheering at the end of the song had one voice, a static static. We could stay out until the streetlights came on. The streetlights came on. We raced our shadows between pools of light. The gibbous globes, dabbed with black paint during the war, were caught glowing softly in the black branches of the leafing trees.

33

I took a job five hundred miles from home. Five hundred miles was what the odometer ticked off as I drove the Dodge Dart from Fort Wayne out to Iowa on old U.S. 30. It took twelve hours with pit stops, the time it would take to run three or four races around the track in Indianapolis. As I drove, I imagined unspooling the concrete of the Speedway, shaking out the kinks of its turns and stretching it straight out behind me. I lost WOWO somewhere near the finish, swallowed in the local chatter of interfering frequencies. At night, though, I heard the edges of it when I was at the edge of sleep. I imagined a pulsating bleat of energy springing from its tower near my old home, the ex-panding circle of the signal opening from ground zero and rolling to-ward me. On the edge of sleep, just below hearing, the engine of my own body, the rush of blood in my ear, circulating.

THE GREEN HOURS

RICK BASS

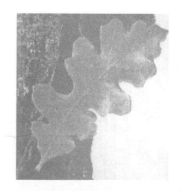

IF I MAY BEGIN WITH ONE OF THE MOST ANCIENT OF CLICHÉS, *it's been a long winter,* I hope you will forgive me. I live on a million-acre island in northern Montana. A cold, wide, deep mountain river bounds me to the south, as does Idaho's castle wall of mountains to the west and Canada's clear-cuts to the north. I am bordered on the east by a vast lake, like a moat. My valley is an island, and within the cold and snowy year, here in Canada's shadow, June is its own island within that island. It's not quite as if you've been sleeping, in all the previous months—nor after June passes so quickly, like a flame, will you immediately close down your year, and begin preparing for hibernation—but it is not until June arrives that you realize, without having understood it earlier, that this is what some relatively huge part of the winter-ravaged husk of your body and soul has been waiting for: the long reach of days, the barefootedness, and the extravagance of warmth, warmth in the north country; and every cell in your body drinks in, absorbs, that new long light, clamors for it, as if you are sipping champagne from some tall fluted glass.

Each year it is as if you have never felt warmth before.

There have been cycles going on all along, an infinitude of cycles—sheets and braids and overlays and intertwinings of cycles (rise and fall, birth and death, motion and stasis)—but in June, so illuminated and heightened are the dramas of these cycles that they are visible even to our often benumbed senses.

They are more than noticeable. They are—in June—dominant.

Beyond the new warmth, and the tongues of gold light, and the tongues of green flame, the thing that most announces itself in the drama of these heightened cycles is the deer. At first they too are as luxuriant as any of us; like us, they too pass through the new light with seeming wonderment. Hugely pregnant, the does wander through the standing water in the marsh, pausing to browse the newly emergent subaquatic vegetation that might carry four hundred times as much calcium as do the dryland plants.

So rich is this diet, at their time of year—the first of June—that the deer will be shitting a stream of clearish fluid into the marsh even as they are feeding on that new growth in the marsh, so that you realize it is as if the slack-water marsh has been given a current by the sun's energy and is flowing now like a stream, passing straight through the deer, as if through an empty vessel, though at least that calcium is transferred to the deer, calcium deposited as if scorched into the deer while all else rushes past. Calcium is of course the one thing the deer most need at this one time of year, this one week—and it is not the marsh that is moving like a current, but, rather, the deer moving through the marsh, that is the current...

I think that deer are to this valley what salmon are to the Northwest: they have their own lives and passages, but they are also immensely, dramatically, a key part of the larger picture, the larger pulse, of this place. Just as the salmon gather nutrients from far out at sea, packing those nutrients into the slabs of their flesh in the form of rich, dense protein, and then ferrying that protein inland, upriver during the spawn where the bears and eagles and ravens and lions and every other carnivore capture and eat that protein and then carry it in their bodies farther inland, up into the mountains, depositing in that manner, in their spoor, deep-sea salmon atop an inland mountaintop, so too are this valley's white-tailed deer the bearers of dense protein, slabs of nutrients moving muscularly from one improbable place to the next, in braids and ribbons—from a marsh plant drunk on sunlight to a deep cedar forest, to a lion's belly, to a sunny ridge in the mountains: a passage, a narrative, for which there is never any end, only new beginnings, always all over again, for as long as there is sunlight in June, and deer...

Early into June, hiking down the trail to the waterfall—flailing at the mosquitoes that form their own braid or sheath around this north country—the season's first hummingbird follows me, following my red shirt through the old forest, down by the rushing creek.

Around this same time—it can happen as early as the first or second day of June—the green cottonwood buds, swollen and turgid with the quick rush of chlorophyll, will begin shedding their heavy, sugary, resinous husks as the leaves emerge, looking like nothing else so much as the green tips of candle flame (entire trees alighting in this manner, like candelabras). And if you are standing beneath one of these trees late in the afternoon, you can hear the sound all around you of the heavy, sticky bud husks falling to the forest floor, pattering like rain onto the forest's carpet of last autumn's dried, yellow-brown leaves, and as you listen, beneath the blue sky, to that rainlike sound of the leaves being born—sticky husks landing on you, bouncing off you like hail—you can scent the exquisite odor of their emergence, and there is no other smell like it in the northern Rockies, no other smell like it in the world, when the cottonwoods begin to breathe, and to exhale their sweet green breath into the valley.

Later into June, not too much later, on an even warmer and windier day, you will be walking along a rushing creek, and will stop with amazement as the sky before you fills with swirling white feathers and flakes. The temperature might be eighty degrees, the wind warm and from the south—the cottonwoods have just released their seeds, their cotton—you know this, you remember it from this time last year, and the year before, and the year before, but so ass-whipped are you still from winter's brute and sun-cheap passage that you physically flinch at the sight of what appears to be more damn snow, snow in June, even on a hot, windy afternoon...

Shortly into June—usually within those first couple of days, as the sticky green pods of cottonwood resin are oozing and pattering to the ground, and as the cries of warblers, vireos, and red-winged blackbirds return (the snipe have been here a long time already, wind-winnowing)—the deer disappear, as if they have left the country.

They simply vanish, like guests leaving a party too early—and you know that they have gone off into the most remote places, the safest, shadiest, most hidden places, to begin preparing to give birth to the fawns, which, having been conceived back during the falling snows of November, were then carried across the long perils of the sleeping winter: crossing all the way across the warming spring, finally, safely, into the tumultuous country of June.

The world knows the fawns are born before you do. Sometimes you'll be fortunate enough to see one newly emerged, knock-legged and groggy, legs still unfolding from that long sleeping passage—but usually it is not until a day or two later that you know all through the forest the fawns are being born. You generally don't yet see the fawns themselves, but see instead their little button-sized hooves, still black and shiny, undigested in the piles of scat left behind by the bears and wolves and lions and coyotes that have been feasting upon them.

Soon enough, the predators will stop catching so many fawns; soon enough, the fawns will be big enough and strong enough to escape. It is only in those first few days, when most of the fawns are born all at once, that they are so vulnerable. Prey swamping, it's called, an evolutionary mechanism that ensures some fawns will survive by sheer mathematical probability—the lions and coyotes are too busy eating this sudden bounty to catch them all.

The world tells you of the fawns' arrival too with the sound of the ravens. The sky is much more active with them, their black shapes flying through the dense forests of spruce and fir with greater agitation and purpose, and their raucous cawings, particularly in the heat of the day, when normally they are silent, tells you of the ravens' excitement, and you understand that they are traveling to and from the many kills, hoping to feed upon a scrap or two, though rarely is anything left, only the sound of the ravens flying overhead, circling and swarming the lion, or wolf, or bear, or coyote, that is eating that fawn...

You can tell also when the fawns are being born, I think, because the same legions of mosquitoes that have been swarming you for the last couple of weeks are one day suddenly bloated. They've been feasting on the defenseless fawns for the last few days, and now when you swat them, there's usually a splash of red on your arm—blood from their last meal, deer blood.

Later that night, on the grill outside, I'll find myself cooking a venison steak taken from a deer the previous autumn. How we struggle to continue to try to believe in the myth that not everything in the world revolves around the consumption of another thing, even as time itself gnaws at the world equally, the animate and the inanimate, the living and the unliving. How we labor to believe that for a moment, or a few moments—as during the high pendulum of solstice or equinox—things can and do exist outside the embattled realm of the utilitarian and the manipulated. How we treasure and cherish the peaceful occasions, too few in number, when we gaze upon something without evaluating its cost or its usefulness: without evaluating it at all, only gaze upon it.

Sometimes in the mountains, I will come upon a bear or an elk from behind, and will observe them looking off a ridge through the trees at the valley far below and beyond, and it will seem to me for the moment in which I watch them unobserved that they are considering nothing, only watching the view of the valley below.

And then a shift in the breeze, or some other sense or impulse, will seize them, and they will know that even as they are watching, they are also being watched—the bear or elk will whirl, will discover me, and in wild alarm will gallop down off the ridge and into the timber, crashing through dry sticks and breaking branches, as the world resumes again its unfathomable but lovely forward motion...

Landscape can be a kind of body, and the rains and snows, and the streams of sunlight, the creeks and rivers and marshes, and the wild lives of the animals that filter through these forests, can be like a kind of blood, drawing a community together as close as if by blood, with all its attendant fidelities and frustrations, the inexplicable passionate loves and fights. As the red blood that passes through a family connects one to the other, so too does the integrity of this landscape, with its many complex workings, pass through and around us all, binding us.

You can see this while standing by the side of a lake, watching the mosquitoes swarm; watching the fish in that lake cruising the surface, sucking down those dancing sunlit clouds, water splashing. You might cast out into those fish, might catch one and take it home and clean it and eat it. If you did, you would be eating the flesh of the fish that had eaten the mosquitoes that had been living on the blood of deer and ourselves, ourselves who had been living on the blood of the deer from last autumn's harvest.

It's enough to make you dizzy. It's enough to make you fall down in the high green grass and call out in some sort of surrender—as if all your life you have been struggling to hold up some false idea of how you fit into the world.

It's like waking up to realize someone, or something, loves you.

The tender fury of June! Nearly every little thing, every tiny thing, is born in June. Even as the world is swelling to its full and busy drama, the tiny world-to-come is murmuring beneath the grass, wandering and creeping and plotting and planning for the world-to-come; for the next wave, and the next. Little yellow grouse chicks the size of Ping-Pong balls scuttle through the forest, following their mothers. Salamanders the size of fingernail clippings wriggle beneath damp leaves, barely larger than mosquito larvae.

The needles on the larch trees, those ancient, primitive trees that are both one thing and yet another—the world's only deciduous conifer—are just now beginning to grow, surging on the sudden leap of June sunlight, even though in ten to twelve weeks they will be done growing, will be dying already, gold by August, or September at the latest...The larch attack the summer with their vigor and beauty, like a man and a woman who have been told they have only one day left to live, and in June (and every other month) all the rest of the forest acknowledges their strength and beauty and bravery...

By the second week of June, as the soil begins to warm, on a hot day when all else is momentarily still and silent, you can hear beneath the new heat a rasping, grinding sound coming from the fields and the forests—coming from the soil, is what it sounds like—and you can spend hours down on your hands and knees searching for its provenance without ever finding it.

It sounds like croaking frogs, or a strange kind of cricket, yet it's strangely disembodied; it's all around you. Whatever it is, there must be thousands of them, and sometimes even as you are down on your hands and knees, parting the grass to search for the rasping sound— lifting rocks and peering under them, and stalking the sound—the tenor and directional flow of the sound will change, so that now it seems to be coming from above you, from up in the trees. It's as if the forest is shouting, or at least grinding its teeth, and it's extremely unsettling.

It's sawyer beetles, doing their best to eat the world.

In his book *The World of Northern Evergreens,* E. C. Prelou describes the mechanics of the sound:

> You are most likely to hear it if you go into recently cut-over conifer forests while the logs are still on the ground. If the logs have been there for any length of time, they will almost certainly contain immature sawyer beetles, voracious grubs with no legs but strong jaws. The steady, rhythmical sawing sound of their chewing is easily heard from as far as ten meters. On a hot, windless summer afternoon, when the birds are silent and (except to a naturalist) the cut-over land seems lifeless, the only evidence of active life may be the sawing sound of the sawyer grubs, steadily chewing wood with the relentless regularity of metronomes.

And what of our lives? Are there always subterranean disintegrations, reverse currents of disassembly, moving beneath us, even in green June? Even as one thing is being built, is another being torn down?

Can such sound be detected? Or in June—green, wet June—do such gnawings cease, in our own scattered and confused lives, bringing us the momentary peace that early summer is so adept at delivering?

I think it is the latter. In June, when I lie in bed at night, in the cool evening, and muse upon, and look forward to, the rest of the summer, and the rest of my life, I can hear no subterranean gnawings. I can hear only the chorus of the frogs, down in the marsh, and the snipe, up in the stars, and the owls booming, down in the old forest. I can hear only the here and now.

By the fourteenth of June, the scent of the wild roses is in full roar—perhaps my second-favorite fragrance of summer, next to the green cottonwoods—and around this time of month, the days are often filled with alternating passes of thundershowers followed by intense sunlight, so that the effect on the roses is that of being in a greenhouse; each new thunderstorm waters the roses, summoning brighter colors and denser odors, and then each new appearance of the sun lifts the petals of the blossoms slightly farther apart, releases a new wave of scent, and the sun-warmed air currents carry the odor in that clean-washed air just a little farther, until by the end of a day of such intermittent rainstorms and sun passages, the scent of the wild roses is so strong as to be intoxicating, as fulsome as a large meal.

What I like best, with regard to the roses, is the way some of them smell when they are next to a cliff, or a talus slope, or a rock wall. I love rocks and stones, and because the roses prosper in rocky, fast-draining places, I'll often find a tangle of scented roses nestled amid a tangle of rocks, and my happiness will be doubled.

As well, the rocks act as a reservoir for extra heat, so that with that refracted heat they help elicit even more odor from the roses in their vicinity: a rose growing out of a rock wall is always going to smell stronger, more wonderful, on a sunny day, than a rose growing any-where else—and again, it's a cliché, but sometimes passing by such places I'll pause, feeling intoxicated, and might even lean in against that rock cliff or rock wall for a moment, dizzy—leaning in against it as if for support, or to worship it.

And if it is this intense for our dull senses, what must it be like for the animals?

Often the rose blossoms, still studded and sparkling with rain from the day's earlier shower, will be humming, shaking, as round bumble-bees burrow into the heart of the rose, busy as a lover, and the sun will be warm against the back of your neck, so that you understand clearly the one basic gospel of all this activity, all this music and noise: that the gospel is heat, heat, the driving force of change—the thing that has been missing for so long, but that is finally here, once more, and right on time.

Other things you can count on, in June: the rich scent of lupine, blaz-ing so royal-blue beneath the old larch that you understand, perhaps for the first time, that blue *does* have a scent, or at least that particu-lar deep shade of blue, in this particular forest. It is a sweet smell, yet so dense that that night as you undress you can still smell it in your clothes.

Heat and rain, heat and rain, are what lift June, in this forest, from the wreck of winter. No month passes quicker up here, despite the absurd lengthening of June's days. (June growing like a crop, like those green fields leaping into grassy flame; June leaping past us like the bucks' antlers in June, which, still sheathed in velvet, can grow as much as an inch a day, as the deer feed on the richness of those newly emerging plants.)

If you do not hold on to your reason, you might for a moment become confused, watching the deer browsing the fast-growing bush, whose shape is almost identical to the fast-growing branching of antlers—the bush shaking as the deer browses among it, the antlers shaking, as the deer nibbles and chews—and for a loosened moment, off-balance by the drama of gentle June, you might feel again that you are falling, even as the curtain of grass leaps quickly up and past you. And up in the north country, the first time you encounter this feeling, you're a little bereft, initially, feeling fooled as the old belief in which the world has instructed you—that you, we, all of us, are huge and important, significant and dramatic and creative and daring—falls away like a small, brown coin dropped into the middle of that field of rising grass...

In subsequent years, if you survive—and accept the shock of that initial surprise, you will still be thrown off-balance by it—June's whooshing, singing, scented, bright-colored arrival, you'll take pleasure in the reminder of your invisibility; you'll be comforted by the graves of grass, graves of shouting, stretching life leaping up all around you, with your own life so small and sedate and safe by comparison that it is as it should be; that you are like a mouse down at the bottom of that cool green, waving grass, hopelessly lost, hopelessly safe beneath the huge mystery and motion and uproar of the world above and beyond...

You can smell the grass growing, in June. You can smell the shafts of sunlight piercing the translucent blades of grass.

You can smell all the forests' different odors as they cool and settle in the forest in pools and eddies, later in the day, as the light grows soft. Cooling lupine, cooling chlorophyll, cooling cottonwood. Spruce, fir, tamarack. Cooling yarrow, cooling sedges. Owls hollering, down by the marsh, and back in the old forest, beyond. Snipe.

Sometime around the seventeenth of June, the first wisps of panic are first able to be scented. In the beginning, it's not even so much actual panic as much as the idea of panic: a dawning awareness of how truly fast June is moving.

Oh my God, you think, one morning around the seventeenth or eighteenth of June, waking up to it like a middle-aged life, or a middle-aged marriage, or a feeling like sleeping late, awakening at nine or ten to find the morning half-gone, and the day itself considerably reduced.

You can't keep pace with June. No one can keep pace with June. It's this realization of the distance between reality and desire that conspires in you one morning to cause you to sit bolt upright and exclaim, *My God, where is it going?* or *My God, it's going so fast.*

Relax. Later into June—almost into July—you will begin to take naps. After the initial panic, you realize how truly long the days hang, in June. It's true, by the third week of June, nearing the solstice, there are only nine weeks of summer left. But more than half a year's worth of light will be crammed into that sleepy, dense richness, in the nine weeks to come. There's no hurry. You can slow down. You can pretend that there's no hurry, can pretend it until you will it into becoming the truth, and it's true, there is no hurry. You can make it be so simply by wishing—in June, at least.

Rain, heat, rain, heat—the two elements alternating like the twin hooves of some prancing animal, drumming upon the land, then summoning the grass, raising it higher each time. On a walk down an old, abandoned logging road, you stop beside a puddle and notice the dozens of baby salamanders, barely larger than these commas, resting in the sun-warmed water. You lift one out of the water on the tip of your finger and hold it up close to your face, so that you can see it. Even embryonic, almost humanly so, its sleek body is muscular, and appears to be tensed, as if ready to spring back into its puddle, as if ready to leap back into the forest. You stare at it, and it stares back at you, unblinking. Its gold eye looks back at you, beholds you steadily, as if looking through the lens of the millennia, or as if watching you from the moon. You're a little spooked by the hint of sentience in a creature you can barely even see. You set it down carefully back into its puddle and walk on, huge-footed.

The solstice comes and goes. It's an absurdly long day. You think of those sawyer beetles, chewing, gnawing, breaking those logs down, crumbling from within.

My daughters and I go for a hike through the old forest, the ancient forest, along a rushing creek not far from our home. We walk for a long time, passing through shafts of late-afternoon summer light filtering in beams and columns down through the latticework branches of old cedars, light falling softly through the feathers of the old larch, and later in the day, on the walk back, the four-year-old, Lowry, asks, seemingly from out of nowhere, *Where is God?*

The question catches me for half a step, maybe longer.

Everywhere, I answer.

Lowry considers this, looks around, then points to a huge cedar. *Is that tree him?*

Yes.

Where's his ear?

Well—he really doesn't have ears. I can see her considering an earless visage, and so I change tack, and fall back on the familiar: *Everywhere.*

She peruses the woods more closely. A tree has fallen across the trail and been sawed into pieces by the trail crew, and shoved to one side.

Is that cut-down tree him?

Yes.

On the drive home, once we get to the gravel drive, I let Low sit in my lap and steer. As she does so this time, I notice that she keeps looking out her window and flashing her pretty smile, and holding it for several seconds. When I ask her what she's doing, she says, *Smiling at the trees.*

It's very late into the month now. I'm sitting in my cabin, working on this essay in the broad daylight, looking out the window occasionally at the green marsh, and beyond that, at the dark-blue of the old forest. The day is shining—no deer are out in the marsh, midday as it is, and the marsh grasses are stirring in the breeze only slightly, moving like the gentle swells of the ocean, far out at sea, as if something immense is passing by, just under the surface—and the climbing heat of the day is lifting the metal roof of my cabin, as the metal expands ever so slightly.

The metal is beginning to creak beneath the sun, making a steady ticking sound, as if trying to register or quantify the sun's warmth, and so accustomed am I to inhabiting this place—this chair, this desk, this cabin—that I soon find myself lulled, as if by hypnosis, into comfortable rhythm with the ticking roof, so that my heart is beating in slow and steady resonance with it, even pausing or skipping, sometimes, as my heart lingers for half a moment, waiting for that next tick, as if waiting for or seeking permission from something—the sun—for each next beat.

For just a moment, an image comes to me of me stepping outside myself; for just a moment, I can imagine a person, a man, like myself, sitting in that cabin, his heart beating in unison with the midsummer sun—sitting in that dark, cool cabin, beneath that green metal roof, which is swathed in shady-green, glowing alder light—and in that image, the man is imagining, dreaming, writing, dreaming with his heart lifting, ticking to the pulse of the sun.

With great difficulty—again, as if hypnotized—I pull back from the image, and willfully turn my back on the man, and the scene of him at his desk, writing. I must hurry outside, and into that rare light and warmth. There are scant hours left.

A JOURNAL
OF JULY

DIANE GLANCY

...a pattern I remembered
from odd pieces of an old family quilt.
Then bringing it finally back against
the darkness of my cheek.
July.
— "The Book of Lowilva,"
in *What Nature,* by Steve Fay

AUTHOR'S NOTE: WHAT FOLLOWS IS A JOURNAL OF DAYS I KEPT
while teaching at the Bread Loaf School of English at the Native American Preparatory School, near Rowe, New Mexico. I'd driven the 2,562 miles here from St. Paul in six days, stopping first in Atlanta for a writers' conference, then again in Memphis, then Elk City, Oklahoma, before arriving here, where I would teach for the month fourteen graduate students in Native American literature, and twelve in fiction.

(1) THURSDAY

My memories of July are darkness in which a large pinwheel of light spins, nailed to the tree by my father. This was the Fourth of July beside which all others would fizzle. Even later, at huge fireworks displays on the Arkansas River in Tulsa, or at the capitol in St. Paul to which whole cities came, it was in the yard of our small house in Kansas City where the definitive Fourth took place. Given me by my father.

And this month I am more than halfway to being a grandparent.

Father, this July is still yours.

The faculty give readings in River House, where I am staying. I was first. Afterward, everyone talked about going to a roadhouse named El Alto, but I chose not to go. I couldn't get to sleep, so I got out of bed, made comments on the student stories, and read assigned stories from *Sudden Fiction* and *Best American Short Stories* 1993.

There. How July begins.

(2) FRIDAY

July as landscape. I woke in the morning in a house at the bottom of a dirt road overlooking the Pecos River. The land is pale green because there has been rain, but the heat is rising. The pinyons and fir, cedar, pine, spruce, and juniper are a darker green.

A mouse greeted me on the step when I opened the front door, and a bird flew under the porch roof. I walked to the eating hall, and felt the sun on the top of my head. It's an uphill walk, and soon I was out of breath in the seven-thousand-foot altitude.

I like the southwestern architecture: the adobe, beamed ceilings, carved doors and tile. The round fireplaces in each room.

I have the headmaster's house, River House; I have two rooms, one for sleeping, one for working. There's a gathering room, kitchen, and then the rest of the house below. I am alone in the house, except when the headmaster comes in now and then. Usually he's on the road raising funds for the Native American Preparatory School.

They say rain will come soon. They call it the monsoon season. But I have my doubts a monsoon will find its way here.

(3) SATURDAY

Outside the other room, the sleeping room, there's a small courtyard with four small aspen trees against a red adobe wall. I watched the shade dance on the carpet. The dance of shade. Squash bloom by the road. Lavender. Trumpet vine. Honeysuckle. Those delicious flowers I don't know.

I made the long walk up the steep dirt road to breakfast. I spent some of the day getting organized, maybe even wasting time after the hectic schedule of getting here and starting up the summer. Then I worked on my Native American literature course. A short burst of rain in the afternoon. Afterward, it was cooler for a while.

In the Native American literature course, we are reading Native American literature. An anthology. Already there are questions: What is an Indian? What is literature? Why is this particular literature uncomfortable? (Already students want to read other, more "entertaining" books, and vote to add *The Lone Ranger* and *Tonto Fist Fight in Heaven* to the reading list.) How do we get beyond stereotype and romanticism? What do we live for? Where does evil come from?

I answered the easy question first: you get beyond idealization by reading the diverse voices in the anthology, from Elias Boudinot (Cherokee) who argued for assimilation in 1826, to Debra Calling Thunder (Arapaho) who wrote about generations of traditional life. Boudinot: "There are three things of late occurrence. First: The invention of letters. Second. The translation of the New Testament into Cherokee. And Third. The organization of a Government." Calling Thunder: "The buffalo sang to us, and their song was our life.... The buffalo sang to us so that we would grow strong. And the Old People would gather together many words to make prayers to the Creator. They would gather words as they walked a sacred path across the Earth, leaving nothing behind but prayers and offerings."

How can you reconcile the differing Indian voices?

It is the same with other voices in the same chapter (in the whole book, for that matter): Yellow Wolf (Nez Perce), after a vision quest in 1869: "It was the Spirit of a wolf that appeared to me. Yellowlike in color, it sort of floated in the air. Like a human being it talked to me. And gave me its power." Charles Eastman (Santee Sioux) after witnessing the massacre at Wounded Knee in 1891: "All this was a severe ordeal for one who had so lately put all his faith in the Christian love and lofty ideals of the white man."

Between 1789 and 1871, there were 370 treaties made, according to Trout.

I moved to the next easiest question: what is literature? My travel dictionary, *Webster's School and Office,* defines it as a body of writing with merit without defining *merit,* but I suppose it means the effective use of literary technique, character, plot, theme until all the parts transcend to some human condition.

Trout calls her book *Native American LITERATURE,* but it's historical document, one of the students says. It just repeats the myths without the voice, the drama. There's no author here. Well, sometimes there is. Some of the pieces are livelier than others. But the students want to read novels. But novels are limited in giving voice to the Native American experience, I say. Can you see literature as many voices in relationship to others, telling a complicated and diverse story of a people that were here when the Spaniards and other Europeans came? Can you see literature as a process of recovery? Can you see it as stories through their own words? A containment of the heart, which would be otherwise lost in grief? Broken and unentertaining as Native life itself? Can you change your expectations? Knowing that the meaning of yourself is bound up in the meaning you find in the literature?

Then came the question I'm not sure how to address: what do we live for? According to the Fundamentalist Bible Belt: to make a decision for Jesus Christ. In a traditional Indian way, it is to survive, to struggle for survivance (Gerald Vizenor's word, meaning survival with meaning). To move from being a human being to Human Being, with responsibility to one's family, tribe, and land.

I have always had opposite roads to follow. One toward a knowledge of Christ (who is a person, a living being, and not a denomination), the other toward an understanding of the way a heritage has worked: a reciprocity in the relational working of the universe.

Maybe this is all tied in with the hardest question: where does evil come from? It seems to come from inside. I am born with a self-will that is defiant in the face of God's will, or even his very existence.

Do good and evil exist as opposite forces? Are they two parts of the same? Is evil relative?

Most Indians don't believe in evil, but ask about their conquest or, as Trout calls it, their extermination. Was that an evil done to them? Certainly not in the opinion of the Seventh Cavalry.

There are dichotomies, inconsistencies, conflicts, inherent contradictions in every culture. In Christianity itself. When Israel crossed the Red Sea and entered the land of Canaan, the land was full of tribes. The Canaanites, Hittites, Perizzites. Israel had God's blessing in exterminating those peoples of the land. This God of love, mercy, justice.

Well, welcome to the literature. I don't have many answers here. Nothing is simple. Not much is clear. You will be as uncomfortable as I am.

(4) SUNDAY

I am usually at my brother's place on the Lake of the Ozarks in Missouri for the Fourth; my son-in-law dazzles us with his fireworks display, launching them into the night air. This year, I am in New Mexico, and Jennifer and Scott stay in Kansas City.

As Muriel Rukeyser says in *The Life of Poetry*, "that most excellent invention, America." I buy a small flag at Target in Sante Fe, hang it on the front door of River House.

Today I went to Laguna Pueblo with students for a feast day. It is the three hundredth anniversary of the mission. A two-and-a-half-hour drive from Rowe, south on Interstate 25, past Albuquerque to Laguna on Interstate 40 West. There we watched the dancers in the plaza, went inside the mission church on the hill, ate, walked past the booths, returned to the school.

That night, after student readings, which are always on Sunday nights, I stood on the balcony of River House and saw a few fireworks over the hills in the distance.

I thought of the contradiction of celebrating the Fourth at an Indian pueblo, of what America's independence meant to the Native American.

The one question I didn't answer: what is an Indian?

I think of my father. Of that pinwheel of light inside darkness.

(5) MONDAY

Hot again. It seems right I spend winter in Minnesota, summer in New Mexico. I'm still reading for the Native American literature class this afternoon. I will be reading the anthology all summer.

As I walked up the hot and steep dirt road to the eating hall, I saw dark clouds to the south. I was eating lunch when the storm broke loose. It rained for nearly an hour. Torrents. Hail. Reddish brown water rushed in the arroyo by the eating hall. I thought of my car with its open windows, parked at River House. I waited until two o'clock, time for my class to meet. We've started meeting in River House because the room where we were scheduled was too hot. I saw a student coming up the walk. He asked if I needed a ride. Everyone was waiting at River House.

The students read from various sections of chapter 4. I got through the Trail of Tears, through the massacre of Black Kettle at the Washita River in Oklahoma, through Sand Creek. But when a student read how, during the Long March, the soldiers killed sheep right in front of the Navajo, I began to cry. It continued from time to time as students read of Chief Joseph in Montana, and of Wounded Knee.

Maybe open grief keeps you humble. It is something I hate to do, but the emotion is overwhelming.

After class, I took the floor mats out of my car and tried to soak up the water with towels. It will take a while to dry out. I left the windows down, and soon it poured again. That night, I drove to the Monday-night movies, the car fogged up because of all the water.

(6) TUESDAY

I woke at four in the morning. Something was in the room. I listened and soon I heard it again. I turned on the light, sat up. A mouse running around the edge of the room, then under the bed. When I looked for it, I saw the bottom of the box spring was torn. The mouse is hiding somewhere in the bed. I got my pillow and clock and moved to the other room, but didn't sleep again.

At breakfast, I asked for a mousetrap.

I came back to River House and worked. I have so much I want to write; I made a list because lists are something you need to make. Also quotes from other writers. Questions. You present, then reflect, is the philosophy of essay writing.

But I've been wrapped in fiction. I want to write poetry—that attic space above where you live.

Someone in class said that poetry is looking at the negative of a photograph; therefore, fiction must be the photograph itself.

(7) WEDNESDAY

Sometimes at night, I hear a noise, a low roar. There's a machine working somewhere. It reverberates in my ear; some of the sound seems to come from within. But when I walk to the eating hall, I can hear the noise coming over the hill to the west where there's a rock quarry.

On a walk near River House, I saw large paw prints and the scat. What kind of animals are around here? I thought the bears were farther north, near San Ysidro; mountain lion, cougar, fox, coyote? This is wild country, someone from New Mexico told me at lunch.

As I sat on the deck and read for class, I saw two crows fly over the valley. When I first saw them soaring over the valley after I arrived here, I cried. Maybe the exhaustion of the long trip, the loneliness.

There is the satisfaction of good discussions in classes.

Tonight I have fourteen papers to read and grade for the Native American literature class.

(8) THURSDAY

In April, Václav Havel visited Macalester College, where I teach, and spoke on "the Civil Society." For some reason, I dreamed about him, and woke in the morning remembering the dream, thinking how strange dreams are. I liked Havel's talk, the pageantry of his visit. But why would I remember him in a dream?

Maybe because I haven't seen the news since I left St. Paul. I wonder if the world is still there. Maybe because the American flag is still on the front door of River House. Maybe because we're talking about America and its history in Native American literature class.

Later in the day, in my afternoon fiction workshop, one of the students was responsible for the writing exercise. She said, write down a dream you had. The dream returned, but now I couldn't remember who it was of. I wrote: I saw someone in my dream. Who was he? I'm trying to remember. I saw him again, I thought. It's someone I have seen before. I remembered who it was when I woke, but now, later this afternoon, I can't. He wasn't directly connected to my life, yet I think I had to send him something, and there he was showing up in my dream to receive it. It was business, not personal. There was a park. I think of the reddish brown color of adobe. He was crossing the lawn with his hand out. When we sleep we go ahead of ourselves like a scout before a tribe. Like the hunters before the women with their hide scrapers.

Later, I remembered: Václav with his adobe hair. I even have a copy of his talk in one of the file boxes I had buckled in the car for my trip here.

"Civil society is an intricately structured, very fragile, sometimes even slightly mysterious organism that grew for decades, if not centuries, out of a natural development, reflecting the continuous evolution of the human mind and morality, the degree of societal knowledge and self-knowledge, and a certain type of civic awareness and self-confidence." No, it does not happen overnight.

Havel had a handle on the struggle of nations. He had seen the saucepan boiling over.

Tonight, students again invited some of the faculty to El Alto. When I asked how to get there, they said I will get there if I'm meant to show up.

I drove there with two other faculty who know where the place is.

(9) FRIDAY

I walked up the hill for breakfast. Two days ago, a herd of cows came into the meadow that climbs upward from the Pecos to the main part of the campus, and this morning as I walked through, the mothers mooed to their calves to get up from resting at the side of the road where I passed. The calves stood and ran to their mothers. I also noticed—what is it?—with horns? A bull? Yes. I saw him watching me from the corner of my eye. It is a bull.

How territorial are they? I asked in the eating hall.

No, he won't charge, they say. But as I walked back to River House, the men from the Preparatory School arrived in their trucks to herd the cows, calves, and that bull back across the Pecos.

It rains all afternoon, while I grade papers.

(10) SATURDAY

Today I drove into Sante Fe to the shoe repair. I also had lunch in Albuquerque with an old friend. In the evening, I started on another group of papers.

I had a call from Jennifer, my daughter in Kansas City, in my phone messages. She and Scott are expecting their first child in October. She is thirty-one, and I've waited a long time for a grandchild. When they told me, I was elated. I remember screaming into the phone. Yet, of course, somehow in the joy, the weight of responsibility hit me also. This will change your life forever, I said. She's a career woman, an attorney with a heavy briefcase, and now will have a child and diaper bag to carry.

Blossom

You remember the pinata we bought when you were in the 4th grade? A lamb with curled strips of paper for wool.

We kept her a while, even named her
and when she had our heart,
we took her to school for your birthday party
where they hit her and hit her.
We watched, crying, at the brutal blows of their sticks
until she broke open
spilling her candy,
spilling.

(11) SUNDAY

What is Indian identity? Certainly, involvement with the culture. But when you give the culture up, as my father did, it does not leave, though you live far from the Indian community and are actually uncomfortable with it, or feel yourself an outsider, like someone you used to date and left without explanation. You feel you still owe them something.

Subversions exist because the Indian text is found between the texts of disputes, and is a paradigm of hyperrealism: the vertical reality of white culture on orbiculate Native thought. Language is a story of the underlying, tough areas of essay.

There, down by the Pecos, I am listening to this moment. Resistance of the rocks in the stream is one of the reasons for noise.

(12) MONDAY

A man named Emilio Arauxo from Galicia, Spain, that land of troubadours, as he calls it, e-mailed before I left St. Paul. He asked some questions about poetry, which I answered. Now he writes a letter with seven more questions about poetry, which I like:

1. What is your experience of the language? Does the poem invent another language inside the language?

Language places us in the world. Language is the land on which I live. There is a Native American belief that our stories can't be separated from the land, but in the case of the Cherokee who were removed from the original place of their stories in the Southeast, and forced to march west on the Trail of Tears, something else has to occur: either a belief that stories move also, or we carry them within us;

in other words, the land is an attitude or place located in the mind. The geography of thought. Otherwise, we are left without stories.

Yes, there is another language inside the language of the poem. I have already mentioned it: it is a geographical location in the abstract; the abstraction of landscape that the language of the poem establishes and attaches itself to.

2. How do you define your attitude toward practice of the performance?

I like to give readings, and often do. I don't know what I think of performance. I have seen poetry "performed," but I just read my words until they leave me and go off to the listeners. I like dramatic readers, but I do not (cannot) read that way. I read my words with the plain spoken voice and hope they form some sort of magic by the very act of transformation from the page to the voice. (You know there is a belief that the voice is sacred, and writing "kills" the voice.)

3. And what would you say of the function of poetry? The poetry like cure, repair, liturgy, exorcism, revelation, charm thought...?

Charm is my favorite of the above words. Like calling a cobra from its basket by the magic of voice (instead of flute). All the evils come out and dance. By evils, I mean poetry calls us from the mundane and unmagical to show us what we can aim for.

4. And how does poetry express nature, landscape, or even the country? How does poetry express space?

By having its being in the space of the page on which it's written. The space of the spoken word as it travels from the mouth to the ear of another and creates a new space in the mind.

5. What is the role of experience and experimentation in your poetry?

I think I write from ordinary experience—the struggle to get to that other meaning that lives on the other side of the hill than fiction. I feel experimentation is important because it captures the fragmentation of Native experience.

6. And what solution do you contribute to the integration of the other arts in the poetry?

I believe in the music of the sound of words, and in the visual art of imagery the words make. I think I contribute to the understanding of the mixed-blood, assimilated voice. I try to get away from romanticizing Native life. I have known the plainness of it, yet I come away transfixed.

7. Does the poem stand alone with its mystery?

Yes.

(1 3) TUESDAY

This morning, as I started down the hill after breakfast, I saw a rattlesnake crossing the road. I stopped. Backed up slowly. He was brown, probably three to four feet long. At the top of the hill, a small dirt road goes to the left, to the laundry building, and there's another road from it down to River House, forming a large triangle around the snake stretched across the road. I took it.

I think he was daydreaming as he crossed the road. He just ambled slowly on as I backed away.

(1 4) WEDNESDAY — BASTILLE DAY

July 14th, the day of my mother's death in 1986. This is the thirteenth year of her death. My father's mother also died on July 14th.

My car tags expire in July. One of the errands I had to run before I left Minnesota was to drive the car north of St. Paul to the inspection station to see if it would pass emissions. It did. The new tags arrived with other mail in a large manila envelope, and I put the new oo tags on my car. I like my license plate: BLZ 949. BLZ for a Minnesota blizzard.

I also mail a letter and pay some bills. My car insurance is also due this month. And AAA — everything, it seems, that has to do with my car.

(1 5) THURSDAY

"I speak many languages. I discuss many things," Raven says in chapter 7 in the James Welch piece "The Marriage of Red Paint and White Man's Dog," from his historical novel *Fools Crow*. I don't know the difference between ravens and crows, but those same two have been flying over the valley since I arrived. They sit on the roof outside the deck of the lower bedroom and squawk. Sometimes I speak to them. "I even speak with the swift silver people who live in the water," Welch's Raven says, "but they are dumb."

Two colleagues tell me how the crows had a metal ring of some sort and fought over it on the roof early one morning. One colleague said when she looked up through the skylight, the crows were looking down at her.

"They're doing it for you," I told her. "They watch us. They've seen the basketball games on the court. They can play too."

I heard the crows this morning. I had set a bag of trash out by the front gate to be picked up, and they got into it. I saw one on the wall outside the upper bedroom holding something with his foot, picking at it with the beak, cawing while doing all that. I stood watching him, knowing he comes from a tribe of tricksters. Knowing he is wise. "I have lived among you many times in my travels," he says. The crow is an old trickster, an observer, a mimic. He shows us ourselves.

At dinner, a student had a story of seeing a mountain lion at the Pecos.

(1 6) FRIDAY

Today was the trip to Trinity Site, White Sands Missile Range, all of us piled into a Preparatory School van and five cars, one of them mine. Four hours south on I-25; four hours back. My 1991 Ford Taurus turned ninety-eight thousand miles. We stopped first at the Atomic Energy Museum at Kirtland Air Force Base in Albuquerque, where in our guide's voice I could hear the smug bravado I remember from the '50s, when America could do no wrong. "We tricked them," the guide said. "They thought the *Enola Gay* was just another U.S. weather plane that made a daily flight over Japan."

We continued south past Socorro and left I-25 at Highway 380, which we followed about seventeen miles to the Stallion Gate of the White Sands Missile Range, where we turned west. We showed car registration and insurance at the checkpoint. After some instructions and the signing of a waiver that said we realized this was a missile range and there were missiles and explosives in the area, and that the government would not be responsible if we got hurt, we followed the guide in his official U.S. Government vehicle, a pewter Suburban.

Fifty-one thousand, five hundred acres, declared a national historic landmark in 1975.

We drove half an hour through the desert north of the Oscura Mountain Range to Trinity, a large, fenced circle. In the center was an obelisk just taller than a man, made of volcanic rock.

The booklet the guide gave us said, "Though radiation levels are low, some feel any extra exposure should be avoided. The decision is yours."

We all entered.

July 16, 1945. Fifty-four years ago today. They opened the site just for us. Somebody knows somebody; otherwise, the site is open to the public only the first Saturdays of October and April.

Trinitite is desert sand turned into a green, glassy rock from the heat of the blast. Most of it was cleaned up, but bits of it remain. "Do not pick it up," the booklet reads. Trinitite is still radioactive, but one of the students picked up a small piece and put it on the booklet I held. I opened the booklet, put the tiny green glass inside, then decided to leave it there. But I touched it.

There had been another hard rainstorm at Rowe while we were gone. Mud was islanded in front of the wooden gates of River House. No way around it. So I walked through it, watching the dark yard. I hadn't left the front lights on when I left this morning, but a motion-detector floodlight came on as I made my way up to the gate, and here I was, blasted white with light, stunned at the surprise of all this light.

(1 7) SATURDAY

July 17th, my brother's birthday. Born in 1944 mid–WW II. I remember my mother at the curb more than fifty years ago, getting into the car, heavy with the weight of my brother, time for him to be born.

"North American," my brother said when I called. He's a meat broker who works from his phone on the Lake of the Ozarks. He sells carcasses of beef. He's a middleman.

There was the leg of a small animal in the road as I walked up to the eating hall for breakfast, reminded again of that violent country of nature.

It rained all evening. I drove up to the eating hall, the road rutted where dirt had washed out between the rocks (some of it down to the front of River House). One of the skylights drips into a tin plant holder, a loud plop with each drop.

I don't doubt monsoon season anymore.

(18) SUNDAY

Once after visiting my son years ago in Texas—he's thirty-four and teaches Spanish at Cedar Hill High School south of Dallas—I passed a truck and horse trailer. Later, I pulled in to a rest stop, and as I got out of the car, the truck and trailer passed, and I heard a bang bang. The horse was kicking his foot against the trailer, wanting out.

I feel that bang. It's the horse within me.

There was traffic on the highway, I said at breakfast. Once in a while we relive our journeys to the school in New Mexico. I'm not sure why. Both lanes had been full of cars and trucks; they were constant headed the other way too.

When I was a girl, we drove from Kansas City to California. There were a few other long trips, a few transfers to several midwestern towns. Maybe that's why a sense of travel is my landscape.

(19) MONDAY

"Seventy percent of the Native American class is mad at you," a student said.

"I'd call it more like a hundred," I said back. Now I have to have a conference with each student. After I turned back their papers, they announced they had talked among themselves. They felt I graded too hard. That I wasn't clear on what I wanted.

The grades they are disgruntled about: A (1), A– (1), B+ (4), B (4), B– (4).

They said they felt set up. That I gave them freedom, then marked them down when their papers didn't link to the literature like I wanted, or if I thought they were redundant in talking about their own sense of identity/heritage/culture, or when their paper didn't hold together for me, or when they didn't synthesize the different parts. Or whatever.

So: Here is their next assignment:

> I want four pages, titled, numbered, double-spaced.
> I want a sense of discovery, a point reached, a connection
>   made to otherness (defined in your own terms).

I want to see information disseminated into your own work
and in your own words.
I want to find structural completeness from the beginning to
end.
All directions should point to the center (the theme).
All disharmony (imbalance) should be in harmony.
Be experimental and risky if you wish.
I want to feel a connection or recognition of something you've
come across in your thinking during readings or class dis-
cussions.
I want to feel a struggle with (or for) ideas.
I like to see the inherent contradictions discussed (the impor-
tance of the community over self, yet self is talked about
in most of the literature we read, though the term "literature" has been debated).
I want to hear your voice saying not what it thinks it should
say, but what it wants to say.
I want to hear a creation myth for your voice, using a different way of thinking than you have before.
I want to see you leading, not me thinking (or coming up
with) where it is you're going.
I expect you to carry through with the expectations you set
up.
I want you to say, this is where we are going, and then take
the reader there. I don't want to be let down.

("It's hard to trust yourself," the A student said during the conference.)

Freedom is harder than receiving direct directions.
I want you to face your paper with respect. I want you to
act like it is bigger than you.
I want to see you rise to meet it.
That is all.

After class, in the evening, I packed and got ready to leave for
three days. In the morning, I have an 8:50 flight from Albuquerque
to Rhinelander, Wisconsin, with a stop in Minneapolis. I'm an hour

and a half from Albuquerque, and have to find the long-term park-and-shuttle to the airport once I get there. I'm giving the noon forum on Wednesday and an evening workshop at the University of Wisconsin's School of the Arts. When I booked all this, I asked why I had to be gone three days for two short programs on the same day (I get back to the Albuquerque airport at 10:16 P.M. on Thursday) and was told I was flying on the university's frequent-flyer miles and have no choice.

I called my friend in Albuquerque and decided to stay there overnight, so I wouldn't have to make the early morning trip from Rowe.

(20) TUESDAY

This isn't my home, I think as I land in Minnesota.

But I'm not sure where home is.

(21) WEDNESDAY

A full day. I was picked up and driven to the school at 7:30 A.M., sat in on a fiction class, then sat in on a creative-nonfiction class, making comments and answering questions in both. Then I sat in on poetry, had time for a slice of cantaloupe for lunch. I read from my novella, *The Closets of Heaven,* for the noon forum, then attended another poetry class. Then an early dinner with the teacher of both poetry classes. One hour at the hotel before my 7:00–9:00 P.M. workshop.

Just like the old Oklahoma Arts Council days in the 1980s: five to six classes filled with students, one after another.

Every book I brought with me or sent ahead sells. For once I have an audience.

(22) THURSDAY

I made the 9:15 A.M. standby out of Rhinelander, and looked down from the Masaba link flight over green and damp Wisconsin. What a change from brown and dry Albuquerque. I also made the 11:25 standby from Minneapolis, and got to Albuquerque about 1:00 P.M. instead of 10:16 at night.

Stopped at Target, then drove nearly two hours north of Albuquerque to the school. It got cooler in the mountains.

The transparency of travel. The things that pass through. The change in landscape. The landscape as travel. The topography of movement. Momentum. Not available to my ancestors is why I hear them say, go.

Driving here, I'd seen the highway streaked with red, and thought at first an animal had been killed, but it was the red-brown Oklahoma soil that had spilled from a construction truck. I have a jar of that soil on my mantel in St. Paul. At the poetry conference in Atlanta, one of the table decorations was a small jar of their red-brown soil. I was the only one who wanted it. It looks like the same red soil in Oklahoma. From red soil to red soil: the Trail of Tears.

(23) FRIDAY

The students' papers from Native American literature are waiting.

Back to River House. Inside the front door, in a large inset window, is a statue of a stylized woman, nearly life-size, the quarter moon looking up her skirt. Maybe she is the sun and there is some old story of the sun (female) and the moon (her brother).

(24) SATURDAY

I spend the whole day reading papers for my Native American literature class. I finish reading the anthology. The grades: A (3), A– (6), B+ (5). I think one B+ should have been a B. Maybe two. Then I would have made one A– a B+. Grading is arbitrary. A judgment call. Subject to pressure. Maybe I should have shifted them all down one place.

I look through Scott Momaday's *House Made of Dawn* because this is the place it was written.

In the evening, I work on one of the novels I brought with me.

The school seems deserted. Everyone has gone to the Spanish market in Sante Fe or on other excursions. But I don't want to go anywhere.

(25) SUNDAY

Once in his life a man ought to concentrate his mind upon the remembered earth, I believe. He ought to give himself up to a

particular landscape in his experience, to look at it from as many
angles as he can, to wonder about, to dwell upon it.
—N. Scott Momaday, *The Man Made of Words*

I remember many landscapes when I was growing up. Places in the
woods, a copse of trees where I would play.

One trip, when we lived in Indianapolis, was to one of the state
parks. Turkey Run, maybe. We were with neighbors. I don't know
what happened, but it was a day of connection to the land, to the trees,
the leaves, the whatever that was there. It connected directly to my
sense of being.

I read and wrote in the morning. By afternoon I had a headache
from eye strain. I drove into Sante Fe to the Spanish market. Bought
a Storyteller for my sister-in-law.

Later on the phone, I heard how hot it was in Kansas City, Dallas,
Minnesota. I remember the hot summer of 1988, when I moved to
St. Paul. The one day of rain in August was when I was loading the
U-Haul.

(26) MONDAY

In the morning, I work. In the afternoon, I pass back the papers in
Native American literature. I feel there is dissatisfaction over the remarks I made.

I feel my headache come back.

(27) TUESDAY

Once again, I spent the morning working. I read. I wrote. After the
afternoon fiction workshop, I went to the Fenn Gallery in Sante Fe
with the whole group from Bread Loaf–New Mexico for a reception.
We stopped at Harry's Road House just north of Sante Fe for dinner.

A former teacher at BL-NM was there. He told me about the Spirit
Woman, La Llorowa, who lives in River House. I asked another colleague if this were true. Yes, she's there, he says. You can hear her
wailing at night.

I drove home under a brilliant moon, so bright there were no stars
on the hour-long trip back to school.

I was sitting in bed reading about eleven when I heard the voices. Only I thought they were coyotes. Eerie, barking, cawing, cackling voices, somewhere in the valley.

I turned the light off. I was tired anyway. I still heard the coyotes. The wind in the pinyons and junipers outside the deck. The roof shaking with wind.

I don't feel fear. Maybe I should.

(28) WEDNESDAY

In the morning I went into Sante Fe, the post office, the shoe repair, Target, Dillards. I bought snacks for the Friday-night reading, got back in time for lunch.

"Did you hear anything last night?" the colleague asked as he sat across from me at the table.

"Yes, I did, but I think it was coyotes," I said. "Is there anything else you're going to tell me?"

He told me there are spirits down by the Pecos. "The wind carries them. The pinyons."

"But I don't feel afraid, not yet anyway."

"They're good spirits," he said. "They're discerning. You aren't mean."

I heard knocking in the house again in the afternoon. It seemed funny this time.

We had a discussion about the Trickster in Native American literature. It is anything with the attribute of duality. Anything that steps outside boundaries. Christianity. Alcohol. Depending on which way you take it.

What a precarious balance survival is.

(29) THURSDAY

She is left without a name
along with two sisters and seven brothers.
She was in a house,
a wind came and blew the house down upon them.
Her death is a few words, and Job, her father, continues to wrestle with
    himself. Later other sons and daughters were born to Job and his wife.
Did they ever think of their first children?

Photographs in the attic of Job's house are taken from too far away,
    their faces left in the distance, the boxes of their belongings at the
    curb for pick up.

Maybe a doll, a toy she wasn't ready to give up.

What utterance could she have said? Was she gone before she had a
    chance
to think of God, and what did she think? They were eating and drinking
    in
the brother's house. They all chose to be together.

She is one who passed nameless in a house blown down on itself.

Was she human existence before thought or discourse? Had she yet
    written?
Had she married? Was she a young woman before life, before thought,
    taken
while she was not yet thinking of questions, of suffering that would beset
her father, before she could speak, or had children, or grappled with
anything while she was eating and drinking in her brother's house,
    suddenly
gone as if she wasn't there? Did she question God when she stood
    before him?
Was she a rebel? A rich man's spoiled daughter, angry she couldn't go
    on eating and drinking?

(30) FRIDAY

I come from a history of stockyards: railroad tracks, old, brick,
warehouselike buildings, wood floors, meat carts with their metal
wheels making grooves. The cattle divided part by part, the hunt
industrialized.

I've wanted to write in the voice of an animal: On a bright morning taken to a pen smaller than the one eaten in; the room at the top
of the ramp; the sudden knife cutting the throat that could have made
sound. The hooks and chains. Maybe we just thought we were walking in line, and smelled, what was it?

Yes, they knew they would die, my father said, but it was quick, mercifully quick. Soundless at least, because vocal cords were cut. Maybe it's why the kill was on the second floor: for the ascent heavenward.

I make another trip to Sante Fe. I can read only so long.

(31) SATURDAY

I drove 169 miles to Cuba, New Mexico, to visit a student, a senior at the Preparatory School who might be considering Macalester. When I talked to his mother, I told her I knew to turn off I-25 near Albuquerque, but how far is it after that? About 65 miles, she said. So it was a day's trip there and back.

I have two days of classes left: Native American literature on Monday, fiction on Tuesday. Then graduation is on Thursday. After my reading that first night here, the seniors asked me to give the final address at graduation. We'll see if they've changed their minds.

And now I'm thinking about the short story. Students want a definition, and I'll tell them a good one tells us a little of what we know a lot about. A short story is about someone who is going through an experience from which they will learn something, I will tell them. A short story is something in which the reader discovers another layer of reality under the one on the page. A story is a little medicine bundle of magic. A grandmother's quilt that carries stories of the pieces of materials she used.

A character who wants something, and something gets in the way. Usually, I'll tell them, you.

And what do I want them to get? A splaying of meaning. Just as poetry comes from somewhere between the upper and lower mind, so does fiction. There is plot, action, character, theme. What it transcends to is an experience of reading and understanding that opens up possibilities.

This magic box of possibility. This calendar of events. This summation of something beyond the parts.

The electricity of recognition of symbol, of portent, of the layers a story should have.

But oh how much relies on interpretation. On you.

I remember wondering what I wanted to do this summer in Native American literature, and remember wanting this: 1) to remember, 2) to envision a future, 3) to make sense of tradition, 4) of acculturation, 5) combinations of both, 6) of walking in two worlds — maybe several worlds.

And I wanted to know what the students might make of them. How they might piece together a quilt of their own understanding.

I wanted to hear as many voices as possible. I wanted to hear their answers.

But what did I think otherness was? What did I think Native American literature is?

Only this: there are no answers, but what you make for yourself.

Here are two crows, high above this valley.

Postscript: I finished classes on August 3rd, packed and gave the commencement address August 5th. Afterward, there was a dinner and a mariachi band. I left the next morning for the two-day drive back to Minnesota, those 2,562 miles that might lead to home.

THE ASHES
OF AUGUST

KIM BARNES

LATE-SUMMER LIGHT COMES TO IDAHO'S CLEARWATER CANYON in a wash of color so sweet it's palatable: butterscotch and toffee, caramel and honey. It is as though the high fields of wheat, the darker ravines tangled with blackberry, sumac, and poison ivy, the riverbanks bedded in basalt and shadowed by cottonwood and locust—all have drawn from the arid soil the last threaded rindles of moisture and spun them to gold. By four o'clock, the thermometer outside my kitchen window will read 105. In another three hours, a hot whip of wind, and then those few moments when the wheat beards and brittle leaves, even the river, are gilded in alpenglow. Often my children call me to the window, and even as we watch, the soft brilliance darkens to sepia. But soon there will be the moon, illuminating the bridge that seems to levitate above the pearlescent river. Some nights my family and I spread our blankets on the deck and lie uncovered to trace the stars, to witness the Perseids of August—the shower of meteors so intense we exhaust ourselves pointing and counting, then fall asleep while the sky above us sparks and flares.

Other nights there is no moon or stars, only clouds gathering in the south and the air so close we labor to breathe. "Storm coming," my daughter announces, and we wait for the stillness to give way, for the wind we'll hear first as it pushes across the prairie and down the draws, bringing with it the grit of harvest. Bolts etch the sky, hit the ridges all around us; the thunder cracks above our heads. Perhaps the crop-saving rain will come, or the hail, leaving our garden shredded and bruised. Sometimes, there is nothing but the lightning and thunder, the gale bending the yellow pines to impossible angles, one tree so old and seemingly wise to wind that we watch it as the miners once watched their caged canaries: should the pine ever break, we may do well to seek concrete shelter.

These are the times we huddle together on the couch, mesmerized and alarmed. We know that the storm will pass and that we will find ourselves to have again survived. We know, too, that somewhere around us, the lightning-struck forests have begun to burn; by morning, the canyon will be nearly unseeable, the sunset a smoky vermilion.

The West, Wallace Stegner so famously noted, is defined by its aridity, and this stretch of north Idaho canyon land where I live is no exception. The Clearwater River is the reason for the numerous settlements along its reach as well as those of its tributaries. Logging, mining, agriculture: all are dependent on the presence and ways of water. Fire, too, defines this land, and at no time more than in the month of August, when the early rains of spring have given way to weeks of no measurable precipitation, when the sweet blossoms of syringa and chokecherry have shriveled and fallen, when wild plums hang blistered with ferment. We must go high into the mountains where the snowpack held longest to find huckleberries, our belt-strung buckets banging our legs, our mouths and fingers stained black, and we go prepared to defend ourselves against two things: the bears who share our fondness for fruit, and fire. Our bear defense is little more than loud conversation and an occasional glance toward the perimeters of our patch. For fire, we carry in our pickup a shovel and a water-worthy bucket. If called upon to do so, we could hope to dig a fire line, or drown a few flames if lucky enough to be near a creek or spring.

Born and raised within a fifty-mile radius of where I now live, I have memories of late summer that are infused with fire. As a child growing up in the logging camps of the Clearwater National Forest, I knew August meant that my father would rise at two A.M. to work the dew-damp hours before noon, when a machine-struck spark could set the wilderness ablaze. But no one could mandate the hours ruled by lightning, and with the lightning came the fires—as many as fifty or sixty from one storm—and with the fires came the pleas for volunteers to man the peaveys, buckets, and bulldozers. Often, the loggers were not asked so much as pressed into service, ordered from their sites and sent to the front lines still wearing their calked boots and pants cut short to avoid snags.

Like my father, my uncles had taken up the life of the lumberjack. Our communal camp was a circle of small wooden trailers, out of which each morning my cousins came, still in their pajamas, rubbing the sleep from their eyes. I remember my mother and aunts in those weeks of searing high-altitude heat, how they rose with their husbands and made their biscuits and pies so that the wood-fueled stove might cool before dawn, then loaded a pillowcase with sandwiches, fried pies, jugs of iced tea and Kool-Aid that would chill in the creek. Somewhere just over the ridge the men battled to keep the fires at bay, while my cousins and I explored the cool recesses of the streambed, searching for mussels whose halves spread out like angel wings, prying the translucent periwinkles from their casings to be stabbed onto hooks that would catch the trout we'd have for supper. My sensory memory of those afternoons—the sun on my shoulders, the icy water at my knees, the incense of pine and camas, the image of my mother and aunts lounging with the straps of their swimsuits pulled down, the brush of skin against skin as my cousins sifted the water beside me in their quest for gold—is forever linked with my awareness of the smoke rising in columns only a few miles away, the drone of planes overhead, belly-heavy with retardant, the smell of something dangerous that caused us to lift our faces to the breeze as it shifted. When the men returned, they were red-eyed and weary, smudged with pitch and ash, smelling like coals from the furnace. I watched them drink tumbler after tumbler of iced tea, wondered at the dangers they faced, and thought that I might want to be like them and come home a fighter and a hero.

As a child raised in the woods, I gained my awareness and wariness of fire by way of the stories told by my elders as they sat around the table after dinner, picking their teeth with broom straw, pouring another cup of the stout coffee kept warm atop the cookstove. New fires brought stories of old ones, and so August was full of fire, both distant and near, burning the night horizon, burning the edges of my dreams.

There was the fire of 1910, the one most often remembered by those old enough to have witnessed its destruction, their stories retold by the generations who have sat and listened and seen with their own eyes the scars left across the land. That year, July had come and gone with only .05 inches of rain. Thunderstorms had started spot fires throughout the Clearwater National Forest; the Forest Service and its small force of men, working with little more than shovels and picks, could not hope to suppress so much flame. And then came August, "ominous, sinister, and threatening," according to Forest Service worker Clarence B. Swim's account of that summer. "Dire catastrophe seemed to permeate the very atmosphere. Through the first weeks of August, the sun rose a coppery red ball and passed overhead...as if announcing impending disaster. The air felt close, oppressive, and explosive."[1]

"Ten days of clear summer weather," the old-timers say, "and the forest will burn." No rains came, and the many small fires that crews had been battling for days grew stronger and joined and began a run that would last for weeks. It swept up and down and across the Clearwater drainages: the Lochsa, Warm Springs Creek, Kelly Creek, Hemlock Creek, Cayuse Creek—the Idaho sky was black with ash. One Forest Service veteran, Ralph S. Space, whose written history of the Clearwater Forest contains lively anecdotal recollections, remembers smoke so thick that, as a nine-year-old boy rising to another day of no rain, he could look directly into the sun without hurting his eyes. The chickens, he said, never left their roost.[2]

On August 21, 1910, the wind began to blow, picking up velocity as the sun crested, until the bull pine and white fir swayed and snapped, and the dust rose up from the dirt roads and fields to join the smoke in a dervish of soot and cinder. Men along the fires' perimeters were told to run, get out, it was no use. Some took to the creeks and rivers, pulling their hysterical horses along behind them. (One legend tells of a panicked horse breaking away and racing the fire some fifty miles east to Superior, Montana—and making it.) Others fled northward, subsisting on grouse whose feathers were too burnt for them to fly.

As in any war, many who fought the fires came away scarred, some bearing the marks like badges of courage while others, whose less-than-brave actions in the face of disaster had earned them the coward's stripes, hid themselves in the back rooms of saloons or simply disappeared. One man, part of a group sent to fight the blaze near Avery, Idaho, was so undone by the blistering heat and hurricane roar of the approaching fire that he deserted, pulled his pistol, and shot himself—the only casualty to beset his crew.[3]

One of the heroes was a man named Edward Pulaski. When he found himself and the forty-three men he led cut off from escape, he ordered them into the nearby War Eagle mine, believing the large tunnel their only hope for survival. As the heat rose and the fire ate its way closer, several of the men panicked and threatened to run. Pulaski drew his pistol and forced the men to lie belly down, faces to the ground, where the coolest air would gather. He hung blankets across the tunnel's entrance, dampening them with what water he could, until he fainted. By the time the flames had passed around them, sucking the oxygen from the cavern, replacing it with a scorching, unbreathable wind, five were dead from suffocation. Another man who had chosen to run before Pulaski could stop him was found a short distance away: the rescue party had stepped over him on the way in, thinking the blackened mass a burned log; only on their return trip did they recognize the charred body for what it was. Pulaski had stood strong in the face of events "such as sear the souls of lesser men," declared the Washington, D.C., *Star*.[4] He would go on to become even more famous for his invention bearing his name, the Pulaski—a combination shovel, ax, and mattock that has since become standard equipment for fighters of wildfire.

Pulaski's story is just one of many that came from that time of unimaginable conflagration. For three days and nights the wind howled up the canyons and down the draws, taking the fire with it. The ash, caught by updraft and high current, traveled for thousands of miles before falling in places that most Idahoans had only heard of: in Saskatchewan, Denver, and New York, the air was thick with the detritus of western larch and hemlock; in San Francisco, ships dropped anchor outside the bay and waited for days, unable to sight land through the blue-gray smoke that had drifted south and descended upon the city.[5] Norman Maclean wrote that in his hometown of Missoula, "the street lights had to be turned on in the middle of the afternoon, and curled ashes brushed softly against the lamps as if snow were falling heavily in the heat of August."[6] The "Big Blowup," they call it now, or the "Big Burn"—not one large fire, but 1,736 smaller ones that had come together across the Clearwater Region. By the time it was over, three million acres and many small towns across Idaho and Montana lay in ruins; at least eighty-five people, most of them firefighters, were dead.[7]

The Big Blowup of 1910 was not the last August fire to rage across the Clearwater: 1914, 1919, 1929, 1934—major fires every five to ten years. The fire of 1919 is synonymous in my mind with the North Fork of the Clearwater, where I spent much of my childhood, for it is there, in the middle of the turquoise river, that a small rise of land bears the name Survivor Island. I remember how, aware of its legendary significance, I studied the island each time we passed along the dusty road, how the heart-flutter of danger and adventure filled my chest. What written history I can find records how two packers and their packstrings, two Nez Perce, and several wild animals had found safety from the fire by swimming to the island. But the story I remember has only three characters: an Indian grandfather, his grandson, and a black bear, all secure upon the island as the fire raged by, the winds it generated whipping the water into whitecaps. At some point, the story became embellished with a detail I still can't shake—how the child, emboldened by the success of their escape, wanted to kill the bear, and how the grandfather would not let him. Perhaps the elder understood the mythical ties he and his charge would forever have to that bear; perhaps he believed that nothing else should die in the face of the carnage that surrounded them.

With each year's August, I feel the familiar expectation that comes with the heat and powder-dry dust boiling up from behind the cars and logging trucks. Expectation, anticipation, sometimes fear of what lies just over the horizon—August is a month of waiting for storm, for fire, for rain, for the season to change and pull us away from our gardens, our open windows and doors, back to the contained warmth of the hearth and the bed that comfort us.

Yet some part of me loves the suspense of August, the hot breath of morning whispering the possibility of high drama, the calm and complacency of dog-day afternoons giving way to evening thunderheads brewing along the ridge. Something's afoot, something's about to happen, and I shiver with the sureness of it.

Years when I have lived in town, surrounded by asphalt, concrete, and brick, there was little to fear from the dance of electricity lighting the sky except the loss of electricity itself. Here in the country, on the south-facing slope of the Clearwater Canyon, what surrounds us is something as volatile and menacing as the tinder-dry forest: miles of waist-high grass and thistle the color and texture of straw. Just such desiccated vegetation fueled the flames that killed the men made famous by Norman Maclean's book *Young Men and Fire,* the story of the tragic 1949 Mann Gulch blaze.

We have no rural fire district here; those of us who have chosen to call this small settlement home knows that should a wildfire come our way, we have only our wits to protect us—that and every available gunnysack, shovel, hoe, and tractor the community can provide. All through the summer we watch from our windows as the sun leeches the green from the hills and the color from the sky, and the land takes on a pale translucence. Come August, we have counted the days since no rain, and we know that somewhere a storm is building, perhaps just to the south where the horizontal plane of the Camas Prairie intersects the vertical thrust of the Seven Devils—the mountains whose peaks rise jagged and white through the brown haze of harvest.

We check our flashlights, our candle supply; we fill our bathtubs with water. There will be wind, which will switch the sumac and send the sagebrush busting across the gravel roads; it will tear the limbs from the trees, drop them across the power lines in some part of the county so remote that the service crew will take hours, sometimes days, to locate and repair them. Then comes the lightning, blasting the tops from the tallest pines, striking the poles that carry our phone and electricity. The lights will flicker, then fail; the air conditioner will moan into silence. Pumps that pull the water from the springs will lapse into stillness; our toilets and faucets will gurgle and go dry. If we're lucky, what passes over us will be nothing more than the black raft of storm clouds, and the seconds we count between lightning and thunder will never fall below five. But there have been times when the bolt and jarring crack have come simultaneously, and we have known, then, that the lightning has touched somewhere near us, and that we must watch more carefully now and smell the air and be ready to fight or to run.

The summer of 1998, on just such an evening, we sat at the dinner table with my in-laws, who had arrived from Illinois for a weeklong visit. My husband, Bob, and I had each kept an eye on the clouds mushrooming behind Angel Ridge; to my midwestern relatives, the oppressive humidity seemed nothing unusual, but to us, accustomed to zero percent air moisture, the too still air signaled a weather change. When I stepped out onto the deck, I could hear the wind coming, huffing its way up the canyon like a steam engine. Within minutes, I was hit with a blast of hot air, then felt the cool come in behind it. The first reverberating boom made the hair stand up on the back of my neck, a response so atavistic I could barely resist the instinctual urge to take shelter. Instead, I raised my face to the wind, redolent of fennel and sage, locust and mullein, the arid incense of a summer's rich dust; along the edges of the breeze, I could smell the dampness of distant rain.

Back at the table, we drank our coffee and shared stories of the past year. I got up once to fill a few pitchers with water. The lightning moved closer—only a few seconds between the flash and thunder—and then a clap so loud and close we all jumped. Not really a clap, not even a boom, but a sharp, ripping roar. Bob and I looked at one another and headed for the porch, and then we could see it: to the west, a narrow column of smoke just beginning to rise. Even as we watched, the column grew thicker, and then we felt the wind gain momentum, pushing east toward us.

The county road, we knew, was our best hope, cutting between us and the fire, providing a fuel-free strip where the flames might falter. Earlier in the summer, Bob had cut, raked, and burned a fire line around our house, decreasing the chances that fire could reach us, but what we couldn't shield ourselves against were the airborne cinders already beginning to descend.

"It's right behind the Bringman place," Bob said. "If we don't get it stopped, they'll be in trouble."

I had a vague acquaintance with Mr. and Mrs. Bringman, a retired couple who have worked the canyon land for decades. Their house and outbuildings sit a quarter-mile above and to the west of us, in the middle of what was then a good crop of ripe wheat. We had come to know them as we have come to know most of our neighbors: by our happenstance run-ins at the P.O. Mr. Bringman is also known for his homemade wine. Local history holds that his land had once belonged to a man of some note who had imported grapevines from France and planted them in the sandy bluffs above the river. "Noble vines," Mr. Bringman pronounced, and we began saving our empty store-bought bottles so that, once a month, he could swing by on his four-wheeler to collect them and drop off a sample of the wine he had put up the past summer, which we dutifully shelved, though he insisted it was quite ready to drink now.

"You get on the phone," Bob said. "I'm going up there." Already the smoke and ash had darkened the sky to a deep shade of gray.

"Wear boots," I said. "Take a wet handkerchief and gloves."

While Bob gathered his gear, I picked up the phone and dialed. Mrs. Bringman's voice came on the line, high-pitched and quavering. "Tell your husband to get here as fast as he can," she said. "Call anyone you can. It's coming our way."

I hung up, then began a series of calls, knowing that for each call I made, two more would go out, word of the lightning strike spreading faster than the fire itself, fanning out across the ridges and high prairie for miles, until every family would be alerted. I knew that every wife and mother would dial the next number down the road, that each man and his oldest sons would don their hats and boots, grab their shovels and buckets and be out the door within minutes, all guided by the pillar of smoke that marked the point of danger as surely as a lighthouse beam.

I paused in my calling long enough to kiss Bob as he hurried out the door. I could see the charge in his eyes, the urgency and excitement, and I felt the regret and longing and resignation I had as a child when the men had gone into the wilderness, to the front where the stories were being made and the dramas played out.

"Remember how fast the fire can move," I said. I had a momentary image of my husband scrabbling across the canyon's steep pitch and felt my heart jerk with fear. "Do you have a lighter?"

Bob nodded, remembering, as I remembered, the story of the ranger who survived the Mann Gulch fire.

"Be careful," I cautioned.

"I will," he said, and was gone.

In *Young Men and Fire,* Norman Maclean researches and describes the August 5, 1949, blaze that caught and killed all but three of the fifteen Forest Service smoke jumpers who had parachuted into the Helena National Forest of Montana. They had been on the ground for less than two hours and were working their way down a hillside toward the fire—an error that would cost them dearly, for a fire racing uphill can easily catch even the fastest man. But what they had found was a simple class C fire, no more than sixty acres. It was a "ground" fire, one the men expected to mean hard work but little danger.[8]

Yet there is always danger when a wildfire is present, and so the crew knew that this one might "crown," as its charred path suggested it had done already before moving back down into undergrowth. The fire that has crowned is what creates the great roar of sound so many survivors describe as the noise of a fast-moving train descending upon them, so loud that communication becomes impossible. A fire such as this may move at about one mile per hour, or it may make a "run" and reach a speed in excess of 150 miles per hour. A crown fire creates its own weather system: the warmer air rises and the cooler air rushes down to replace it, creating a "fire whirl," a moving convection that can fill the air with burning pine cones and limbs, as though the forest itself has exploded. This incendiary debris gives rise to spot fires that can flare behind or in front of the fighters; crews find themselves suddenly surrounded, ringed by fire that seems to have come from nowhere, sprung up from the ground and converging.[9]

With these conditions comes the possibility of the phenomenon firefighters most fear: the "blowup." Blowups occur when fresh air is drawn into the "fire triangle" of flammable material, high temperature, and oxygen. Few have witnessed a true blowup and lived to tell of it, but those who have speak with wonder of the fire's speed. Maclean recounts the experience of fire expert Harry T. Gisborne, perhaps the first to observe, survive, and describe a blowup. The 1929 fire Gisborne detailed occurred in Glacier National Park and burned ninety thousand acres with almost incomprehensible swiftness, demolishing "over two square miles in possibly two minutes, although probably in a minute flat."[10]

The Mann Gulch smoke jumpers were young and had dropped onto a terrain that may have seemed at the time less threatening than the densely wooded ridge in the distance. They were at a point where the tree-studded mountains broke open to grassy plains dried to amber. Perhaps they believed themselves safe amid the loose-rock slope and low-lying vegetation, but they were tragically mistaken. They had their tools—their shovels and Pulaskis—but what they did not have was knowledge of the ways of this fire and of how, within an hour, it would cross the gulch and push them screaming up the steep hill, crest at the top, and die there with them. Bunchgrass, cheat grass, some immature pines mixed in with older growth—these were all that was needed to create the blowup that engulfed the men. Two of the three who survived did so by racing the fire to the ridge and winning; the third, the crew's foreman, saved himself by escape of another kind: instead of running, he stopped, struck a match, set fire to the grass at his feet, then stepped into the flames he had created. He lay facedown on the still-smoking earth, covered his head with his hands, and waited for the main fire to catch and sweep over him. And it did.[11]

A steeply pitched, basalt-strewn slope covered with dry grass and scattered patches of timber—the very terrain Bob was headed into. As I watched him pull away, I prayed that he would have the foreman's presence of mind should the fire overtake him. I could see the flames themselves now, flaring twenty feet into the sky. I let the screen door swing shut, went back to the phone, and began another call.

The men came in their pickups and stock trucks and cars, on their four-wheelers and tractors—a steady parade passing by our house. Having exhausted my list of numbers, I gave up my station to stand with my children and in-laws where our gravel driveway met the gravel road. We tried to determine what we could of the fire's direction. We waved our support as our neighbors flew by, driving too fast, we thought, though we understood their urgency. On the slope just above us, the Goodes and Grimms and Andersons had set their sprinklers atop their roofs, dampening the embers and sparking ash that floated and fell around us like fireflies in the darkening sky. I'd instructed my ten-year-old daughter and eight-year-old son to stand ready with the hose, knowing that should the power lines go down, our electric pump that drew water from the spring below would be useless; our only defense against the fire would be whatever water remained in the storage tank. But if we used that water for prevention, we would have none left should the fire reach us.

As twilight deepened, the fire's glow grew more distinct along the western horizon, until the last rays of sunlight were indistinguishable from the orange-red aura melding sky to land. My mother-in-law, city raised and only half understanding her son's desire to live in such a wild place, did her best to rein in her fear; my father-in-law, nearing eighty, paced in frustration: he should be out there, offering what help he could. Had it not been for the fire's location along the breaks of the canyon, our ability to keep him clear of the battle would have proved much more difficult.

We all knew the immediate danger Bob and the other men faced—the fire—but there were other concerns I kept to myself. Just down the road from our house is a jut of land named Rattlesnake Point: we kill an average of two diamondbacks per year in our yard; the annual score we spy along the roads and paths outside our property we leave be. In times of fire, every living thing flees from what threatens it—cougar, deer, elk, rabbit, pheasant, field mouse, bear, and rattlesnakes, too, slithering ahead of the heat faster than most could imagine, sometimes smoking from their close brush with death. My hope was that, should Bob encounter a snake, it would be too intent on escape to strike at the legs of a man.

And then there was the terrain itself: fragile shelves of talus, slanted fields of scree. The land could give way beneath your feet, begin moving like a tipped mass of marbles. I have had it happen before, while hunting chukar, and found myself grabbing at the smallest outcroppings of sage and buck brush, feeling them pull loose in my hands, the only thing below me a chute toward an outcropping of columnar basalt that would launch me into the canyon. I've always been lucky, able to catch a knob of stable rock or wedge my foot into the roots of a stunted hawthorn, but that memory of falling, of gathering momentum, of hurtling toward endless open space, has never left me. I knew that Bob was surefooted and careful; I knew, too, that in the lapse of light, the ground's definition would fade.

The smoke thickened. We covered our faces with our hands, coughing, our eyes watering, unwilling to abandon our vigil, knowing how much more those closer to the fire were having to endure. I ordered the children back to the house, but they would not go. They wanted to be of some help, perhaps believing, as I did, that our standing guard might somehow keep the fire at bay. The glow had moved higher up the ridge; the flames leapt, receded, then leapt again. With the wind and lack of equipment, we had little hope that simple manpower could contain the fire. I estimated that a half-mile of pastureland separated us from the conflagration—that and the road—and I told myself we could hold our ground for a little while longer before loading the cars with what we most treasured: photographs, books, laptop computer, the children's most precious belongings. The possibility of losing our home and everything in it seemed very real to me, but I considered it with little emotion. What was uppermost in my mind was the safety of my loved ones: the family that gathered closer as the smoke increased, and my husband, somewhere just over the ridge, risking his life to save the nearby houses and barns, the crops and timber, perhaps even an entire small town should the fire run the ridge and drop over into the next draw. At that moment, I wasn't sure the saving was worth the risk. How could I weigh the loss of my husband against nothing more than property and economy? There was little chance that anyone other than the firefighters themselves was in danger—by now, everyone in the county had been warned. Why not stand back, allow the fire to meet the river on one side, the linkage of creeks on the other? In the end, it would burn itself out.

But then I remembered the stories—the fire of 1910, the young men who had died so suddenly by thinking the distance between them and the fire enough—and I realized that this wasn't about the wheat field a mile down the road or the home of the family at the bottom of the draw. It was about fire. It was about crowning and whirls, convection and blowups. It was about August and a summer's long drought. It was about three million acres burned in a matter of days—the width and breadth of many whole states.

What I wished for, then, was the help of all the technology and knowledge such fires of the past had brought into being. The fire of 1910 showed everyone that crews of men scattered about the burning edges would never be enough, and then the Forest Service began its study and transformation of fire fighting. But we do not live in a forest; we live on private land, too distant to warrant the protection of the city, too sparsely populated to afford the luxury of a volunteer fire department. That August of 1998, our situation was little different from the one facing the farmers and loggers and townspeople of 1910: our primitive tools had not changed, and at that moment, I began to realize that our chances of saving our home had not, either.

I moved down the driveway, preparing myself to announce that it was time to pack up, to position ourselves by the river where Bob might find us. But then came the roar of something overhead—the thrum and air-beat of a helicopter. I looked up to see what I had believed would not come to us: help from the outside world.

From beneath the helicopter hung a length of cable attached to a large vinyl-and-canvas bucket. The pilot did not head for the fire but for the river, where he hovered and dropped and filled the bucket with nearly one hundred gallons of water—a half ton hoisted up and swinging from the Bell Jet Ranger. As we watched, the helicopter leaned itself toward the fire's furthest point, the bale opened, and a sheet of water rained down.

My daughter and son let loose with whoops of excitement. My in-laws and I clapped and hugged, jubilant at this unexpected turn of events. Again and again, the pilot followed his path from river to fire, until the ribbon of flame along the horizon had dimmed to a faint glow; within an hour, we could no longer point to even the smallest flare.

We stood watch as night came on, unable to see the helicopter now but tracing its direction by the deep hum that drifted to us on the smoky breeze. Although we were safe, rescued by the graces of the Clearwater–Potlatch Timber Protective Association, who had sent the helicopter because they were fighting no fires of their own, we all knew our wait was not over: somewhere in the darkness was our father, son, and husband. The line of vehicles that had sped by us earlier now came in reverse—a slower-moving column whose lights passed over us as we held up our hands in a gesture of greeting and gratitude.

"Bob will be coming soon," I said. "Let's go make him some fresh iced tea."

We walked the few yards back to the house, turned on the porch light. Our jubilation had been replaced by a quiet fear that grew with each passing minute—fear that receded and then leapt up each time another pickup approached but did not slow and turn into our driveway.

"He should be back by now," my father-in-law said, pacing from the window to the door and back again. "Maybe I should go see if I can find him."

I knew that Bob and the other men would have driven off-road and into the fields, gaining what time they could against the fire. Even if we could locate our four-wheel drive, there was no guarantee Bob would be near it. Without light, the diminishing fire behind him and the total blackness of rural night before him, he could walk for hours before finding his way back to where he had parked.

"I think we should wait," I said. "He'll stay as long as he's needed. Someone will come and get us if there's trouble." I listened to my own words, only half believing. What if Bob had gotten turned around, fallen into a ravine, been isolated and trapped by the fire? What if he were lying somewhere in the dark, injured, unable to save himself?

I thought again of the rough terrain—familiar to me from the many walks Bob and I had taken, the many hours we had spent exploring and visually mapping the area. The fire likely would have eaten its way across Bedrock Canyon, down to the river and up to the top of the ridge, creating acres and acres of charcoal earth, charcoal sky—like a black blizzard. How could we hope to find him?

We made the tea. We gathered and washed the dinner dishes. We distracted the children with books and puzzles until none of us could be distracted any longer. We gathered outside in the cooling air, still heavy with smoke that would hang in the canyon for days.

"Come on, Bob," I whispered to myself. "Come on." I thought of my mother and aunts then, waiting as I waited, fighting the growing panic with the mundane details of daily life. How many hours had they spent watching from the window above the sink, their hands submerged in soapy water, their fingers blindly tracing the knife's edge? How many Augusts had passed in a haze of worry and despair as the lightning came down and the flames rose up and the men disappeared into that place where no one could reach them?

But then, the lights at the top of the driveway, the held breath, the release as the engine idled and died.

I let my daughter and son reach him first, escort him into the house. He was covered with soot, his white T-shirt scorched, burned through in some places; his face was red, nearly blistered beneath the ashy smudges. We hovered around him, offering tea, voicing our concern and sympathy. I stepped up close, breathed in the familiar smell of everything burned—the dead grass and live trees, the cloth on his back, the singed hair.

"I'm so glad you're okay." I wanted to cry—out of relief that he was home, out of anger at the fire, out of frustration that I had found myself caught up in the same cycle that my mother had known so well. I knew that the stories Bob would tell of the fire would become part of our family's shared history, that we would recite and embellish the narrative with each passing summer, that we would always remember the way he shook his head when he told us: "There was no way we were going to be able to stop it. But then I heard the helicopter, directly overhead. I looked up just as the bottom of the bucket opened. I've never felt anything so good in my life."

The next day, we drove downriver to view where the fire had burned—an oily pool spread across the golden hillside. After the fire subsided, Bob had found himself disoriented and had wandered in the dark for an hour before coming across several other men. Together they were able to find their way back. "I can look up there now," he said, "and have no idea where I was."

Later, when I asked my son what he remembered about the fire, he answered quickly: "I remember that I couldn't breathe." My daughter recalled the ash falling and my concern that we would lose our water supply. And she reminded me of something I had forgotten: "What I remember most," she said, "is how badly I wanted to go and help fight the fire, and how you wouldn't let me."

Perhaps she will be the one to leave the phone and go to the place where stories are being made, the one who will not be left behind. One of the most respected smoke-jumping crews in the country is composed entirely of women; of the fourteen Oregon-based firefighters who died in the Colorado fire of 1994, four were female. I shudder with the thought of my son or daughter choosing to try himself, herself, against such an adversary. I wonder if I would come to dread and despise the month I love so well, for I am strangely wedded to the tyrannical heat, the thunderstorms, even the fire—the absolutism, the undeniable presence of August in my life.

Instead of wading the ashes of August, I spend many late-summer days wading the river. This is Nez Perce land, and the water's flux covers and uncovers the remnants of their ancient industry: arrowheads, spear points, blades of obsidian. I come to the Clearwater armed only with a hook and line, meaning to fool the fish with a tuft of feather, a swirl of bright thread. I step in to my waist and feel the strange dissonance of temperature—my feet numbing with cold, the crown of my head hot with sun. I stand for a moment, brace myself. I am all that is still, an island anchored by nothing more than the felt soles of my boots. I load my line, cast toward the calm above the current. I imagine the fish rising, its world a kaleidoscope of shattered light.

Through the cooling nights of fall, during the long nights of winter when ice rimes the eddies, I dream of August, the water at my hips, my line lacing the sun. I wake to the odor of wood smoke—my husband firing the stove—but for a sleepy moment it is the warm wind that I smell, the burning of yellow pine and prairie grass and wheat stubble. I smell summer sage and mullein, the licorice spice of dog fennel. I smell the cool drift of fish-scent off the river. I open my eyes, expecting early light, the windows still open to the morning breeze, but what I see instead is the darkness before sunrise, the frost that glisters each pane of glass, and I am bereft.

1. Stan Cohen and Don Miller, *The Big Burn: The Northwest's Forest Fire of 1910* (Missoula, Mont.: Pictorial Histories Publishing, 1978), 3.

2. Ralph S. Space, *The Clearwater Story: A History of the Clearwater National Forest* (Forest Service USDA, 1964), 96.

3. Stan B. Cohen and A. Richard Guth, *Northern Region: A Pictorial History of the U.S. Forest Service, 1891–1945* (Missoula, Mont.: Pictorial Histories Publishing, 1991), 61; Cohen and Miller, *The Big Burn*, 18–19.

4. Cohen and Miller, *The Big Burn*, 18.

5. Cohen and Guth, *Northern Region*, 58.

6. Norman Maclean, "USFS 1919: The Ranger, the Cook, and a Hole in the Sky," in *A River Runs Through It and Other Stories* (Chicago: University of Chicago Press, 1976), 140.

7. Cohen and Miller, *The Big Burn*, v.

8. Norman Maclean, *Young Men and Fire: A True Story of the Mann Gulch Fire* (Chicago: University of Chicago Press, 1992), 33.

9. Ibid., 34–37.

10. Ibid., 35, 37.

11. Ibid., 74–75, 102–6.

SEPTEMBER

RUNNING IN PLACE

KATHARINE COLES

Aubade

Sky of pearl. Behind me,
my love dreams. Love dreams
mountains hazed with gold.
Hazed with gold, late summer's
canyon opens. Before
me the canyon opens
fall's sky of pearl.

Accidental

1. I move into it
      and the world solidifies—

scorched hill giving to cool
      range, tree to forest—

and keeps giving.
      The way I hold

the expected note
      against its shift,

a kind of ghost,
      in the space between them

a life's sweet pain.
      All horizon,

this dawn I run through,
      summer falling into

afternoon, when he, still
      now sleeping,

will pump his bike
      up this same canyon

while I sit dreaming frescoes
      on ancient walls, colors

brushed white by time's
      long flutter of wings,

walls I walked through, standing
      as if surprised

to find themselves supporting
      no roof, no attic,

no portrait or rack for hanging
      spoons and crockery over

space the archaeologist believes
     burned under food

as if to hurry time.
2. About which we say, *Done.*

Through which water
     still flows

and fire tears, air
     eroding under

that stream giving up
     stillness, leaving

disaster's ghost
     etched on the walls,

no more. Smoke
     pours out windows, empties

into nothing, knots
     my chest. So close

my mind still bellies
     all night under

smoke, pulls
     the plug, turns

the water on, passes
     on danger—while,

3. across a continent, an ocean, fingers
     touched wires, set

the timer, so
     intentional, so gentle, their

precision looked
     like nothing

so much as love, until
     wall came down, floor on floor

collapsed like time;
    until the shoppers, militiamen taking

days off, mothers with strollers
    stepped into that

separate
    space a moment

dismembered, silence
    holding, held

as if dust could stop
    its flight, until the mouth

opened, the first
    scream entering time.

4. Millennia later. The second
    before. I'm still beating

against the world as if it mattered,
    shaking my hair

free of those wings as if
    I could, as he shakes off

the bee—lazed
    coincidence of flight

he's wheeled into—
    and in one gesture's

passing irritation enters
    time's slant

skid
    sideways, wheels holding

his weight it seems forever, then
    wheel folding;

and even as he tells me how
    he got us

here, into emergency,
     my mind slips

his words, grasps
     how space folds—

moment's comprehension,
     the way a bird's color

flutters the eye,
     mind never

composing it into *bird.* Then gone;
     the head

meeting asphalt
     in that moment

thinks, *Gone. I knew this*
     was coming.

5.   Blood.

Flash of green and light
     estranged by chemical

wash, long adrenalin surge
     toward the wail.

I almost had
     control, he says later. I almost

had it, under
     doctor's hands seaming

flesh over bone.
     How many stitches?

I ask, but I think
     emergency room, as if it made

its own space, as if my mind
     could hold one thing,

my lucky life of near
     misses and their ghosts,

and he says
  I almost had it

and I hold his hand, wondering how
  to get the blood

from his long hair,
  his favorite green shirt,

trying not to picture
  earth's dizzy

flash of spoke, how
  soft is bone and tissue

he carries his life in,
  its matter lately

divided, abstracted by numbers,
  bits so minute

they dissolve even my love into
  mere idea (his so

solid shoulder, blood
  on my hand), and I

can no more
  imagine them than

infinity. Which
  they contain.

Late summer, 1998

Picking Blackberries

Noon. Hottest
day turning into
hazed cloister. I eat

fruit gone too far
wild for love's table: deep

gone into ripening's
doze, lopsided, grown
odd-bodied, estranged, but

so sweet, lateness
broken on the tongue.
Where is that

perfected body I keep
reaching under leaf

and thorn to pick? He
dreams on, asail before
the bedroom's machined breeze.

I'm still eating, finding
no berry fine
enough to feed him.

The Double Leash

Blizzard to lilac. Dandelion
to leaf. Endless
variation of seasons I note

in passing, smells
I cannot smell: rotting
gardens, feces, musk of cat.
              These two

run in front of me, golden
shoulder to patchwork, heads
lifted or lowered into

scent, tongues lolling. Ears
damp with their own
spittle and each other's

tell me, tethered a pace behind,
their journey's epic: tipping
forward to the familiar or
stranger's distant yap; angling

to my breathing, whispered
praise, my slightest
suggestion.
        Ignored.
           The shepherd
throws herself into

any whirring wheel, to herd
the neighbor's tractor mower or
the UPS truck's packets
home; pulling her back,

the golden's oblivious
ballast, instinct heading
always for the gutter's

deepest puddle, her own way
within the forked leash's
one-foot range. As we pass,

the clans set up
their barking, as if we
were news, gathering center

of a congenial warning
din—mine answer with
disturbances of pace, an extra pull
or lollop, grins thrown

slant-eyed over shoulders
until one hears a call
she can't ignore, surrenders

to baying's ferocious
joy moving
muscle and bone. Moving
storm, storm's eye: happy

universes whirl in their skins
as I do in mine. Unknowable,
their fate. Mediums between
foreign principalities, they're tied

to me, to each other, by my will,
by love; to that other realm
by song, and tooth, and blood.

Meeting the Moose

1. He's planted roadside when we round the curve—
it is a he—drinking at a runnel.
He doesn't meet us halfway. His rack is small,
but what a weight to bear. Not unnerved—
no time—just alert to my own heart's
beating size and shape, I say, *Stop,*
sit; and for once both dogs drop
as one to watch, twitching tails and ears
so lightly you might not notice, vibrating interest.
He finishes drinking, ambles up the road,
angles his bulk to keep his eye on us,
still unmoving, struck in watchfulness,
as he heaves his great, absorbent body
like miracle up the mountain's sheared-off face.

2. He must be the same one. It's his canyon
our house teeters over, marking precisely
the edge between our sprawl—constructed city's
potted begonias, porch mats, wrought iron—
and the cut a moose can still range through
climbing into wilderness's heights.
That time, five A.M. The only light
the light snow makes, as if cold could glow
like heat through matter. So big I couldn't see him,
only darkness pictured by the pane—
six inches and a single sheet between us—
that would not yield but finally took his form.
He was that calm. He stripped the aspen clean.
His. The shape my palm marked on the glass.

3. Two miles below that curve, the road pitchforks.
Left: up to our street, where our neighbors
tie and net euonymous against deers'
winter starve. Straight: downtown. Right fork—
no surprise—from here it's all downhill:
the capitol's domed proportions, portioned grounds
orderly as law. He sails down,

pauses his great self to think, all
deliberation. Why not that way? Capitol
flowers, so sweet; grass cool and slick.
He makes the news. The senators call him *Bullwinkle*
and pose, until he charges their porticoes,
traps one against the marble, shaking his rack,
forcing a position. Photogenic, unsinkable,

4. he was still bound to lose. A tourist.
His huge knees bend under sedating darts.
Men adjust the cables, test the straps.
They are careful—this is human interest—
how they tie that bulk to carry it
over, into the scenery. Kept in mind
as long as the cameras roll, then gone, behind
our rough horizon. A simple ferry
picks him up, transports him beyond our ken.
Than the moose, we'd rather have memory
blurred by plumbing's hum, car ignitions,
alarms clicking on. What if he wakes then—
the great machine above, a beating aerie
so far from earth, from any kind of heaven?

5. I'd rather think of him haunting this ground
I inhabit between my human life—
no, I must mean my *machine* life—
of picture view, glassed, girdered round—
and my life crossed by leaf and wind,
by water sound, the whir of dog-flushed grouse,
squirrel teasing from within his house
of bark. Both human. Whenever I round that bend,
every time, he still stands in that space,
the absence that is fully, only him
obliterating all with heft and loom.
Perhaps a miracle, that we live in a place
where moose can fly. But only where we send them.
Ever farther. Last time, he walked back home.

The Squirrel

I sprawl flat out in tall grass at roadside, last night's rain soaking into
my back, my head on a rock. Wind washes a sky so blue I know
how fast we are spinning into it. Both dogs, leashes still tied around
my waist, are licking my face. They look only a little sorry. They
forgive me how I keep them. Safe in his tree, the squirrel chatters.
See what can happen? See? See? See?

Storm's Eye

Quiet between these hills, moment
suspends, though overhead
treetops churn, and that hawk plays

a hard fillup of wind. Shifting light,
oak unleaved, dragonfly, blade

of grass—my own mind
spun free by motion
finds this turn suddenly

unfamiliar. I check
my watch, replaced by time,
how it carried my body

here, breath by breath, and now
measures bruised sky. Hawk slips
free the rim just where

yellow stormlight seeps
low between cloud and mountain, light
pressed into such rich resin

I have to stop, cannot stop
looking, stilled by the gaze.

The Glass House

Drawn out all day
to stripped trees, the
alarming vista, the gaze

takes earth's body:
dry peaks, faces' long
slides toward the furrow,

where water works
stone into its bed.
Almost nothing. Only

a breath's lift, the opening
sky draws through
vanishing membranes into

vertigo. Then
light shifts. Bare
duskfall, its moment

touching the house, presses
lamplight inward, turns
the eye on its own face.

After Fever

Under his bush,
invisibly, the grouse
folds his wings, won't flush;

in a week, hoppers
have taken over the grass,
as if they'd waited for

my eyes to turn away.
My step, tentative, still
springs them into flight,

crazy, sideways, light
bodies flung toward
they can't know what

fortune of leaf or flower,
water or pavement's disaster.
They take their chance

as I do, too soon
climbing blue spectacle,
a perfect breeze, out

of body's consumption. How
invisible well-being, worn
like lightest cloth

the wind moves, sheer
exhilaration, over
skin, the world alight

as I come back to it—
how pain is felt
as presence, not the slipping

away from one's own—
the terrible body's weight,
its knowledge, burning out.

Canyon Ghazal

They fall against their rising, cliffs undone
by weather and what weather's left undone.

Sunk at canyon bottom, the road scales
its arched body into lift undone.

And I run within a thunder's pulse
that lights me through, flickering off and on.

What haven't I done? Wind strips the oaks. Limbs
strain at root, by their wild heft undone.

Even the sky can't stop. It gnaws itself,
black cloud undone by black, unloosened one.

What can I do but let the storm trouble
eye and blood, the heart at wrist undone?

Until it's passed, moving me between
nerve and fault. I resist. Undone,

the coal's consumed by its own breath. No rain.
Just trembling air. Sky's whip. The passion done.

Anatomist

The width of the shoulder is 1/4 of the whole. From the joint
of the shoulder to the hand is 1/3, from the parting of the
lips to below the shoulder-blade is one foot.

And if you should have a love for such things you might be
prevented by loathing, and if that did not prevent you,
you might be deterred by the fear of living in the night
hours in the company of corpses.
—da Vinci's notebooks

Dawn. Blade's touch, more gentle
than any lover's, which does not consider

limiting damage, lifting only
skin to lay bare artery, fat from muscle left
intact under eye's dispassion. As if

only the dead deserve
delicacy. Or stone, against which
the chisel tests its measures. Consider

the body flayed, examined as landscape,
furrow and light, the swell cut
fringed with oak, sage, grass long declined

yellow, wind's dry caress
under which I assume earth

holds, though mountains keep
distance so austerely—retreating

even as I move into their perspective—
I almost see the clench, slip of skin

over bone the wind makes whistle.
How this land, for all
its salt and dry and poison, is that much more

made itself. Gluteus maximus
knots into the climb, into rectus
abdominus; knees hinge; every stride

the tiny footbones flex—even
shoulder blades move as if to flight

almost remembered, predicted by flux detailed
centuries ago, by the light

of flame, under hands moving
their own numerable bones. It must

have been like sailing the unknown's
infinite horizons. I could never keep my body

poised in marble readiness,
white muscle holding action

furled almost forever, as if to say
here's what stone means, though it's only art

making that cut, Thoreau of the body
dividing arm into wrist into torso, multiplied
by head, halved height supplemented by

scrotum's length. Da Vinci's constant:
his body speaks down the centuries,
saying *one,* meaning *me,* magic

number translated into flesh,
then stone. As that act withheld
increases power, until

it only erodes, the surface
pocked and smoothed, chiseled limbs

blurred, then thinned, then fallen. We all live
in such company. Bread, sun,
word, dawn air chilled

by water and midnight's ghost: the very lift
of thigh becomes thigh, lung,
and heart, alchemy growing

motion incarnate, blood and flesh that keep
twitching even as the pace winds down.

The Last Day

could be any
one of these: gold
deepening before
blue shadow; wind's

water-rush through leaves;
the world turned out
to soak up late
sunfall. Shade,

no longer holding
air's heat, blades
under trees. Winter's
wedge end edges

between low peaks
and dusk, where light
burns this sweet
ache before dying.

Poetry & Spirituality

Today, the wind rides the thighs of grasshoppers,
and leaves fly like rescue from burning trees
I could almost turn into something. All this talk.

I'm guilty too—me, an unbeliever
raising a miracle, these ungainly hoppers
pelting my chest, my hips, fixing a moment

to my shorts, my footfall opening one
so brilliantly into flight you might think
butterfly, before its wings let it down.

UNDERGROUND

ELIZABETH DODD

Two things are required to truly see.
Love and knowledge.
—Chet Raymo

"Kansas and America"
Some hated slavery
Some hated blacks
Some hated slaves
All loved land
—Michael S. Harper

THE MONTH AFTER THE AUTUMN EQUINOX, WHAT LIES AHEAD?
One year, it's an ice storm on Halloween, killing countless hedgerow
trees between the fields. Another year, the days continue warm, sun
flooded and bright with almost desert light until a sudden spate of
rain sets in, washing over the country roads; along the interstates, the
prairie pastures turn to gray-brown, turbid expanses of marsh, then
shallow lake, while the cars *whish, whish* along, their drivers stiffly
alert. I have a friend who says these are his favorite sorts of days: the
close, forced intimacy of low skies and curtailed visibility; the poignant
solace of long, thoughtful hours indoors. But I think otherwise. It's a
time to be out-of-doors, surveying the surfaces that soon may be
windswept, snow clotted, so cold and hard the mud will hardly crumble underfoot, will hardly show the prints of where you step.

On a hill above Cedar Creek, I look over some rancher's pastureland fenced with scrub-wood posts, stone posts, metal stakes—a pro-
gression of materials. In the steep bank beside the rough and rutted
road, a few roots dangle their fringe along the edge, illustrating something of the unseen life of runners and rhizomes. A neat, dry hole
opens to the southern exposure, the dirt heaped and piled about the
entrance—badger, surely, though there's no other sign I discern of the
furtive animal.

At summer's end, the grasses—big and little bluestem, switchgrass,
Indian grass—begin to transfer nutrients below the soil, so that the
only living part of the plant is well underground, leaving dry, rasping, whispering stalks still standing in the wind. And they shift into

autumn pigment, not the vivid warmth of hardwoods—oaks and maples, say, in the height of fall color—but subtle russet-brown-and-gold. "Strawberry-blond," my friend Anne says. Sometimes a hillside's like a bright-red ale; sometimes it's muted, the shade of leather I keep hoping to find in a pair of shoes. On a cloudy day, the color can be wine dark, blood dark. Sometimes, when the late daylight catches in the drying seed heads or the upper arabesques of grass leaf, it's like an illuminated pelt, the shock of a badger's unexpected, grizzled side, before it turns and hurries out of sight. It's October: Keats weather, full of delight and shiver in the recognition that all this *is,* but cannot last.

The near field, I can see, is almost all Indian grass, tall as my head. Across the road, big bluestem towers even higher than the grass around me. Just this side of a wooded draw, a pair of does lift their heads; they are the color of grass, and watch me moving, solitary and peculiar in my bright jacket.

Another day my friend Janet Throne agrees to join me as I look for Cedar Creek Cemetery, a tiny pioneer graveyard I saw cupped beside the creek bed as I walked atop the hills. It's easier than we both imagine, just half a mile of gravel after we turn onto the county road. We're chatting about time, and time left. Today is the first I've heard that Janet and her husband are considering moving; I think of them as fully rooted here, and I feel my face get wistful while she talks. Once, while my husband was out of town and I was very ill—and realizing why so many people once died of influenza—Janet brought me home-baked bread and lemon Jello. I don't want her to leave.

"Still," she says, "there's so much I want to *do* here."

And already we're pulling up outside the barnyard-style gate. A barbed-wire fence demarks a nice-size square of well-mown grass; three huge cedars lift from among the central cluster of graves. Janet remarks how empty this small graveyard is: "The little cemetery on my parents' land in New York is absolutely full," she says. "There was no more room within the walls."

Here, a chest-high iron fence—no gate—surrounds the graves of David and Rebecca Hays, who came to eastern Kansas in 1854 with their three grown sons. They all staked claims in this area—here, along Cedar Creek and a little farther west on Pfiel Creek. They were among the earliest settlers in Riley and Pottowatomie Counties. We know this from a newspaper clipping Janet has brought along, a little scrap of interest she'd been saving. The slightly yellowed paper tells us the land "once belonged to David Hays and later to his son Samuel. Samuel deeded the land in April 1900 to Blue Township, the officers of which now maintain the cemetery in excellent condition."

Today, however, we find that the settlers' headstones both lie broken on the ground. I climb the iron fence and kneel to look: Rebecca's stone has obviously been vandalized before, and old, dried glue is visible along a ragged edge. It's easy to see how the damage was done: someone brought a footstone, labeled only "Mother," and used it as a hammer stone to break the granite at its base. The hammer stone is dark and smooth except for one corner, where it's freshly chipped.

After I clamber back out from the tiny fenced-off square, we examine the other graves, arrayed to the north of David and Rebecca's wrecked markers. There are some whose names suggest they are unrelated to the Hays progenitors: Amanda Disney (1845–1897), whose stone declares, "Found my husband and children all; From you a mother Christ does call." Two children are remembered with a tall spire of stone: Carrie York (1872–1876) and Elmer F. York (1880–1881); there is no sign of the York parents anywhere. A tiny, hand-hewn stone belongs to Andy Lewis, with no dates or other signs.

Prominent beneath a huge branching cedar is Samuel Hays, whose stone pronounces at its top "Father" and at its base "At rest." "Sam'l Hays" died June 23, 1914, aged eighty-four years, two months. Beside him, symmetrically, is "Mother," whose stone declares, "It is well." She is "Wife of Sam'l Hays," and she died October 17, 1905, at the age of sixty-four years, seven months, and twenty-two days. Her headstone doesn't tell her given name, though a tiny, rectangular footstone bears the initials T. J. H. Her son, Andrew (1865–1913), is buried beside his wife, Della (1866–1956), and two children: Ward, an infant son, and Vance (1906–1949). The farthest grave to the north has a flat slab of marble, level with the ground, imbedded with a bronze plaque identifying Inez Hays (1875–1953). She lies just outside the large corner markers consolidating this third generation of Hayses.

We wonder: Was Inez a stepmother, and the children (remember those great appellations, Father, Mother) set her just outside their family plot? Was she an unmarried daughter of Samuel, someone they'd all kept hoping might yet find a husband?

It's quiet here, but a cow lows from a nearby field, and I'm sure that in spring we could hear the creek from where we stand amid cedar and sunlight, studying these old monuments to otherwise nearly anonymous lives. The air is clear and dry, and this fall already has farmers worried that a dry winter is ahead, a bad beginning for their winter wheat.

"Look," says Janet, with her hand just brushing the nineteenth-century granite, "at the gates on this one. You can hardly see them—" But there they are, finely stenciled, just ajar, through which we might be glimpsing heaven. Despite our wondering, our comments on the workmanship or artistry of the stones, we focus most of our attention on the names and dates, running our fingers along worn letters, tracing out uncertain words. And though she's such a distant, nearly hypothetical stranger, I'm taken with this pioneer woman dead just shy of a century. Though I know she died on the seventeenth of October, I don't know her name. And, suddenly, I want to very much.

Jeanne C. Mithin hands me her card, and sets me down to fill out paperwork declaring who I am and what my interests are. Yes, she can help me. The Riley County Historical Museum has a whole file on the Hays family, and moments later I'm leafing through pages typed on a manual typewriter. Here is information about deeds and land tracts, newspaper obituaries, lists of children and birth dates.

David and Rebecca Hays came to Kansas Territory from Brooke County, Virginia—now located in the northwest tip of West Virginia, just north and east of Wheeling. The story of their journey west is fascinating, perhaps even more so because it is quite sketchy. David and Rebecca, with their youngest son, Samuel (then twenty-three), left in the spring of 1853 and traveled down the Ohio and then up the Mississippi until they reached St. Louis. Robert, their oldest son, met them there, having spent the winter in Cedar County, Iowa, just east of Cedar Rapids. Together the four continued on the Missouri River to Westport Landing at the northeast edge of modern Kansas City, and then went overland to Cass County, Missouri, just south of the city along the Kansas-Missouri line, where the couple's middle son, Joseph, was farming.

Reunited, the family would "await [the] signing of the Kansas-Nebraska Act," wrote Medora Hays Flick, David's granddaughter. That legislation repealed the 1820 Missouri Compromise, whereby slavery had been prohibited throughout most of the Louisiana Purchase. Instead, popular sovereignty — that is, the vote of white male citizens — would determine whether the state would be admitted slave or free. The resulting power struggle escalated tensions, first along the Kansas-Missouri border and then throughout the nation. After a few brief but violent years of conflict in "Bleeding Kansas," John Brown returned east for the October 16, 1859, attack on Harpers Ferry, where he tried to seize a Federal arsenal in order to arm slaves and instigate a great uprising.

President Franklin Pierce signed the Kansas-Nebraska Act on May 30, 1854, but the family did not depart until August 1. They may have been purchasing supplies; they were very likely developing — and enjoying — ties with people in Cass County, since later both Robert and Joseph would marry sisters from the Paul family, whom they had met there. In any event, more than a year after the journey began, on August 1, 1854, David and Joseph came into the territory to stake their claims. David's granddaughter describes their entrance "in a horse drawn wagon, loaded with farm and carpenter tools, seed wheat and provisions for horses and men to locate a home and help make Kansas a Free State." She recounts their route as partially using the new "Fort-to-Fort" road from Fort Leavenworth to Fort Riley and crossing the Kansas River on a pontoon bridge. Then they followed Cedar Creek "to where they found an excellent spring of water, timber and stone for building. Here David located, built his log cabin, broke prairie, sowed wheat, and then he returned to spend the winter."

For much of August, September, and October, the men would have been reshaping this handsome watershed. I imagine them rising with first light, through the oppressive heat of August and September, then in the welcome mellowing of October, when the chilly mornings would have warmed into the days I love most: that russet weather, Indian summer, invigorating and kind to hard labor.

In December, Samuel came to the Cedar Creek claim and joined his brother, establishing himself on land adjoining his father, while Joseph settled farther west, across the Big Blue River in contemporary Riley County. By 1857, David had built a stone house on the land, where he and his wife would live until their deaths. I don't know when Rebecca came to join him; perhaps she waited until spring 1855, and came with her husband and her son Robert—who built his own cabin along Cedar Creek, and became the father of eight children. Medora, whose stories I'm recounting, was the youngest, born in 1873.

Among the typescripts, I find two memoirs in longhand—dated and signed by Medora Hays Flick. Her penmanship is neat and clear and reminds me a little of my mother's. The first of these manuscripts is from 1934 and called "My Grandmother's Story." Again the names come quick and fast, and I have to scratch out little family trees in my notebook, trying to visualize how the narrative plays out amid the teller's sense of kinship—who she is and how her people came to be here. In the spring of 1857, Robert returned to Cass County, Missouri (unfailingly Medora writes this "Cass Co. Mo."), to marry Sarah Emmeline Paul. Sarah had been raised by her mother; Mary Noel Davenport Paul was widowed "when their three children were mere babes," and the story unfolds to show the gutsy strength and resourcefulness of that single parent and her grown daughters.

"When the civil war began in 1861," writes Medora of her grandmother,

> her home was . . . right in the middle of the border warfare. The border ruffians had issued an edict that no "free state" white man should cross the border. My uncle J.W. Paul and Milt Kincaid, to keep from helping raise the Confederate Flag, skipped across in an unguarded spot. After the men came to Kansas, Grandmother insisted on her sister (Mrs. Milt Kincaid) coming to live with her. The border ruffians looted her home and took everything in it. Grandmother traded her farm for a tract of land on the Blue River in Grant Township. . . . She loaded what household equipment she could into an ox wagon drawn by two yokes of oxen, and with her cattle and sheep and two horses she started for Riley County accompanied by her daughter Julia, her daughter-in-law and baby, and her sister and baby. Ephraim Jones (Mrs. J.W. Paul's father) drove the oxen to the Kansas line and was told very emphaticly [sic] he could go no farther.

Of course, the restriction applied only to white men. What did Ephraim do? I wonder. Simply kiss his daughter good-bye, step out of the wagon, and begin to walk back home?

Aunt Jane (Mrs. J.W. Paul) took the whip and drove the oxen. Aunt Julia and Mrs. Kincaid walked and rode the mare Blaze and drove the cattle and sheep. Grandmother and the two babies Mary Kincaid and Charless Paul rode in the wagon. They were two weeks on the road. One yoke of oxen and the unbroken horse was stolen enroute. They bought corn along the road and grated it to make bread. They milked the cows in the morning, strained the milk into the churn, at night when they camped they had buttermilk to make their bread and butter to eat on it.

Some man on horse back passed them and brought my father (Robert Hays) word that the women were on the way. He mounted his horse and went to meet them. They met near St. Mary's and came to our home on Cedar Creek. When they went to their own home, father mother and two children and the Hesea Springer family who had been neighbors in Cass Co. Mo. accompanied them. They gathered wild grapes and grandmother made wild grape dumplings for their dessert.

Already I like Medora very much. I like her voice, her sense of detail in these family histories—really, they are origin myths for the postpioneer community where I live. I enjoy the understated pride in her kinswomen when she says, simply, "Aunt Jane took the whip and drove the oxen."

The old Fort-to-Fort Road they would have traveled to St. Mary's— also called the Great Military Road, which connected Fort Leavenworth on the Missouri River to Fort Riley on the Republican—was in use by 1853–1854. I've walked along a tiny segment where it remains on the west side of town in Warner Park, a large, hilly expanse of native prairie and woody draws deeded to the city by the Warner family, early settlers in the area. At this point running almost directly north to south, the old road—a trail, really—is still visible, and quite recently some local volunteers have erected markers describing the road and its role in the early stages of white immigration into Kansas Territory.

The trail's eastern access lies amid grass and gallery woods, adjacent to what could have been the parking lot for a giant Walmart Superstore; our city council, however, denied the zoning proposal after vigorous and widespread opposition from residents throughout the community. For a couple hundred yards, it's an easy, flat trail under cottonwood trees, although in spring it must have been muddy, slow going along that bottom drainage land. Then quickly the route lifts into steeper going, and bridges and gravel walkways have been added where the ground is severely eroded.

Once out of the cottonwood lowlands, hardwoods shade the way. They're burr oaks and hickories mostly, and on an autumn day one's footing is unsteady with new-fallen nuts. This portion of the road, through "the Wildcat Range of hills" (named for nearby Wildcat Creek), must have been tough going for David and Joseph's wagon loaded with carpentry tools, when they decided to backtrack from Fort Riley to their choice along Cedar Creek. The women of Mary Paul's ensemble didn't come quite this far west, but the route they took from St. Mary's to Cedar Creek has disappeared, lying somewhere in the private land of ranch and farm that stretches east of town.

Some of the oaks along this tree-lined trace are surely old enough to have seen the settlers coming. One in particular is a leviathan, vast and mostly undiminished by rot or age. Once, my husband and I tried to span it with our arms, but just about a foot of bark separated our fingertips as we hugged the trunk—roughly twelve feet around. It's a savanna tree: the heavy, muscular limbs start branching just above our heads, and their lateral reach shows they didn't have to struggle upward to find sunlight; its crown was, and still is, the canopy, though the ground under it has greatly changed.

Medora Hays Flick has more to uncover for me. From within her filed recollections and the other documents that make up the Hays-Flick file, I find the answer to the mystery of "Mother, wife of Sam'l Hays." It has seemed too lonesome—unfairly desolate to have your name effaced from your own tombstone. Unlike her cousins, Medora was scrupulous with her genealogy, recording seemingly endless lists of names and relations.

Aunt Julia (née Paul, who walked and drove the cattle, sheep, and horses) married Joseph on December 24, 1863. Sarah Emmeline married Robert on March 22, 1857. The third son, Samuel, married Termuthis Jane Vance, born in Beaver Creek County, Pennsylvania, on February 15, 1831. Another document in the file surmises, "It is probable that she was the daughter of John and Jane Vance who came from Pennsylvania and settled in Myers Valley just north of Flush [Kansas]."

So this is "Mother," Termuthis Jane (T. J. H. on the tiny footstone marking her grave), who appears in a poor photocopied picture in the file. Her hair is parted in the middle and pulled straight back; her left ear shows from the angle of the camera. She wears a dress of dark background flecked richly with light dots, with a long ruffle at the hem and a light, frilly looking collar circling low around her neck. Her face looks young, serious, with a small mouth and small eyes. Samuel sits beside her, dark bearded, with his left elbow resting behind her right shoulder. She holds a baby, unidentified, on her lap. Her obituary reads: "The death of Mrs. Samuel Hays Saturday afternoon, October 7, has saddened the hearts of her many friends and loved ones. Mrs. Hays had been in failing health for nine years, and last winter took the la grippe which irritated other ailments and ultimately in heart trouble." (Perhaps this explains her tombstone inscription, "It is well.") "She was the mother of twelve children, three boys and nine girls. Ten grew to man and womanhood, who together with her aged husband mourn the departed dead."

Here I also learn that Inez—the low stone just outside the Sam'l Hays family plot—was T. J.'s daughter, the ninth of twelve children. One of our guesses was right: she had never married. She lies buried as a daughter, not a wife or mother. She died the year her cousin, Medora, wrote out her family memoir, "Cedar Creek in the Fifties," for a joint meeting of the Pioneer and Historical Societies.

And here, from Medora's original ink-on-lined-paper manuscript, composed in 1953, I read another brief hint at mystery and answer. "David was a man of strong convictions, religious and political. He was so opposed to slavery, he was part of the 'Under Ground Railroad,' both in Virginia and Kansas."

His granddaughter's description of her other relatives' tense odyssey into Kansas Territory supports this declaration: those men who "skipped across the border" in a spot unguarded by proslave Missourians; a family house looted by "border ruffians." And David and Rebecca may have come from Virginia, a slave state, but it was from the most northern tip, home not to plantation holders but to Unionists who became West Virginians rather than secede. Their home along the Ohio River, where David operated a boatyard, could have been an ideal spot for spiriting slaves into the free North. The Hays-Flick file identifies their son Joseph as having served in the Kansas State Militia, ordered into active duty in the Fourteenth Regiment on October 10, 1864, serving as a corporal. He fought in the "Battle of the Blue" on October 22, 1864, when the Kansas Militia prevented Confederate troops under Gen. Sterling Price from advancing into the state from their position along the border after the Battle of Westport. The militia drove Price down the border to Linn County, where Union general Alfred Pleasonton caught up with the Confederates, in the October 29 Battle of Mine Creek, the largest Civil War battle fought in the Kansas Territory.

"Well," says librarian Jeanne Mithin, her face alive with both interest and skepticism,

> that's the only reference I've ever heard of the Hays family being involved in the Underground Railroad. Of course, there were Abolitionists in this area, people who came from the New England Immigrant Aid Society. But there were also slavery sympathizers: many of the officers at Fort Riley brought slaves with them, and Geary County was originally named Davis County after Jefferson Davis—and it was years and years before the name was changed. So it's hard to say. The truth may have been buried with that generation.

But there are other tantalizing hints. Just west and south of where Cedar Creek meets the Big Blue River, an early settler named Henry Strong is said to have been a stationmaster on the Underground Railroad with a hidden cave on his farm claim, where slaves were concealed by day before being conducted farther north by night. After the war, the Strong family used it as an apple cellar for their orchard; by the 1950s, as the city spread suburban neighborhoods into the area, the cave was filled in with dirt and paved beneath residential Beck Street.

Nearly due east, members of an Abolitionist group, the Beecher Bible and Rifle Company, established themselves as early as 1856, and three miles east of the town of Wabaunsee (home of the Beecher Bible and Rifle Church), Mary and William Mitchell operated a station from their home. All this was well west of the busier "Lane Trail" escape route and the hotbed of activity in Lawrence—the area that drew John Brown and his family, prior to the disastrous attempt at uprising at Harpers Ferry, West Virginia, on October 19, 1859. But there may indeed have been an occasional diversion of fugitives into this part of the territory. The Reverend Charles E. Blood, minister of an area First Congregational Church from 1856 to 1861, is said to have participated as well, conveying slaves up the Blue River Valley to Beatrice, Nebraska.

David might not have been a stationmaster, but he might have helped in some other way, from time to time. ("He was part of the 'Under Ground Railroad,'" is how Medora phrased it when she wrote in 1953.) His homestead on Cedar Creek was only a few miles from Henry Strong's station, across the river. The families might have collaborated; perhaps David conducted fugitives who stayed in the Strong cave.

If the Hays family helped transport runaway slaves, the most important records of those actions would be the memories of those whose lives they touched in brief, portentous moments. Jeanne Mithin thinks that Kansans sometimes claim a larger Abolitionist role for their ancestors than may be warranted, and she's surely right about this: as the Civil War recedes further and further from living memory, we want our connections to that crisis—moral, political, and military— to have been ideal, cut from the mold of civic courage and heroism. I do admire those tough pioneer women who carted their sense of self and household halfway across an imperfect continent, pursuing the life they might yet live. And if they, and their families, hid other families in the bosom of their own conviction, if they fed and dressed— and, sometimes, doctored—people on the deadliest, most earnest journey one could take across such varied, unknown ground, well, we know that some people did all this. The stories now are buried in ways we don't know how to uncover, or recorded in ways we don't know how to read.

I think Toni Morrison is right, in her novel *Beloved,* about the way a black American—a former slave—might have commemorated some aspect of the terrible journey north to Cincinnati, across the Ohio River into freedom. The young slave mother, Sethe, goes into labor while she's still in Kentucky, weak and bleeding from her bare feet and cruelly beaten back. In the woods not far from the river, she meets a runaway indentured servant, a white orphan girl named Amy Denver, who helps her deliver the new baby. It's Sethe's own will and determination that get her to the North, but she memorializes her essential, if tangential, helper: she names the baby Denver.

One hundred and forty years ago, the route through Bleeding Kansas would have been hard, the white settlers still struggling, far from real railroads and their connections to amenities to shape a comfortable life. A hidden cave along the river valley might have been welcomely cool in summer, but surely cold in winter, and lonely, terrifying, in the long hours of waiting until the next leg of travel would begin.

The Blue River today is dammed, and the Tuttle Creek Reservoir stretches north for nearly twenty miles, clear up to the former town of Stockdale, flooding what today's old-timers claim was the prettiest valley around. A couple of towns and cemeteries were relocated to accommodate the rising waters. If slaves slipped north along the Blue, that segment of their journey has been underwater—13,500 surface acres of it—for forty years, the sediment settling to coat and cover the terrain in further weighted darkness.

And here is a final, lovely bit of irony, nothing that can be analyzed as evidence, but it holds for me poetic power: Termuthis (also spelled Thermuthis) was sometimes a given name for women in the 1700s and 1800s. It is said to have been the name of the biblical figure—a pharaoh's daughter—who adopted the baby Moses. It was Moses, we know, who led the enslaved up into freedom.

THE INHERITANCE
OF AUTUMN

JOHN LANE

IN NOVEMBER, MY FATHER WILL BE DEAD FORTY YEARS.

Each year, as the planet cools and the leaves drop across upstate South Carolina, I remember him. In remembering my dead father, I dig with a spade, try to unearth his absence. Lately, this absence has taken on the force of a haunting. I have written a sequence of poems where my father appears to give me advice, correct old habits, finish unfinished business. In my dead father's absence he has become a presence. Through the poems he has come to inhabit this place—Spartanburg, South Carolina—as clearly as we inhabited the town of his death.

November is, for me, what the old Dutch called *Slaght-maand,* or "slaughter month," the time livestock were slain and salted for winter; it's the Saxon *Wind-maand,* or "wind month," when fishermen drew their boats to shore and gave up fishing until the next year.

Attending to the place of November in my own turning year, I often try to imagine my dead father doing something simple, such as peeling the last home-grown cucumber of the season with his pocket knife, watering sunflowers, placing the wedding ring on my mother's finger, or changing the oil in his Willis Jeep at the Southern Pines, North Carolina, service station he ran for years. I too plant sunflowers, and it is too easy to note how they grow huge and yellow all summer, and collapse under migrating songbirds in November, when the lolling heads dry and the seeds fall to the ground.

I can hear the temporary melancholy in the sentences I've just written. It is the sound of November approaching through the ether.

It is the sound of words turning heavy with the coming cold. There is this natural inclination of mine to head off sadness, to make a joke, assure the reader that I am not melancholy, and this is not a melancholy essay.

But what else could be written about November? It is always a darkening month, even in South Carolina. The streetlights come on early, the sheets at bedtime already cool.

My father was born on a farm in coastal North Carolina, before the First World War in deep winter; I was born on the cusp of November in the North Carolina sand hills two hundred miles northeast of here. If my father had not taken his life, my mother would never have moved us back to Spartanburg, this mill town where she grew up. It is my mother's place. My grandparents were married in a church three blocks to my west, but it has become, through time and habit, my place. Without my father's death, I would literally be someplace else today. Without his death, November would curve more easily between October and December.

My father's death placed me psychologically: I am the son of a suicide. I live in a place of abandonment, where the address is always uncertain. The weather is never predictable or steady for the son of a suicide. Out there somewhere on the horizon is the Great Depression. Some sons of suicides (and I am one) are the world's Tom Joads, and every day could end up a dust bowl.

"Father/land," I've written often at the top of a journal page and never been quite sure how to play out the lost drama of place and family and abandonment. Somehow land is part of the pattern for us both. I've always seen him as a man who lost his place. And I'm one who has worked to recover mine through writing. Just this morning, I went through twenty years of journal entries for Novembers past, trying to get some fix on whether I've always been depressed in the fall. It looks as if the answer is no. There were stretches of November where I was in love, or traveling, or writing with great concentration. Other years I have mentioned his absence, though, reflected on our shared space: "Father seems to be my sea," I wrote in 1997. "I'm soaked in it." And just last year: "My father's patterns. What are they?"

Reflection seems, judging from the journals, something I have grown into lately, and this November will be its culmination in some logical way. I was only five when he died. I'm forty-four now, and this month I finally did the math on the back of an envelope: my father was born on January 14, 1915, and he died on November 15, 1959, aged forty-four years, ten months, and one day. On August 29, I was exactly the age of my father when he died.

When November arrives in less than a month, I will be well past him.

Will that settle his death for me? Will it ever be settled? How does one understand a death, any death, much less a father's suicide with no note left behind? I know all the details: my father came back disturbed from World War II and spent time in an army hospital; he unsuccessfully attempted suicide several times in the years from the war until his death; he struggled with depression and alcohol; he finally succeeded in ending his life idling in the driveway of our home in Southern Pines, a vacuum-cleaner hose tucked in the window of the car; my mother found him.

Soon after my father's death my mother moved us back to South Carolina to be near her people. My father's sisters kept in touch through letters and Christmas cards. When I was old enough I knew I would travel on my own to visit my father's family. By 1964, when I turned ten, I rode a Greyhound bus from Spartanburg to Wilson by myself. After my aunts knew I could do it, I went every summer. They paid the ticket—from Spartanburg to Raleigh, and from there, on the local line to Wilson. It took all day. Much of the day I rode through tobacco fields.

My Aunt Eula picked me up at the station in Wilson. She drove a practical white Oldsmobile, called the trunk "the boot." When I opened the door to put my bag in, the cool air in the car smelled of tobacco smoke. Usually Aunt Alice, my Aunt Eula's old-maid younger sister, was with her. My mother had told me how Aunt Alice spent part of her younger life in the state hospital. She said it was because of a man, someone the family did not want her to marry. I knew that a man came to visit her sometimes and always brought intricately carved wood projects he had made himself: a shelf for trinkets, a box for jewelry. Aunt Alice and her suitor sat in the living room of Aunt Eula's house on Greene Street and talked. I bring this up because I've worried about my father's melancholy, my Aunt Alice's stints in the state hospital. Inheritances come in many forms.

It is mostly through his eight brothers and sisters that I filled in my father's life from childhood through marriage. He grew up on an eastern North Carolina tobacco farm that had been in his family for two hundred years, drove a school bus for the county upon graduation from Lane School, a rural school named for his family. Then he tried to farm a crop of tobacco but enlisted in the army as soon as there was a war to take him away.

"Your father never talked about it," my mother always said when I asked her about his war years. I know now that when he left the 146th combat engineers, C Battalion, he was a Tech 5. His unit saw action in North Africa, Sicily, Italy, France, Belgium, and Germany, before finally ending the war in Czechoslovakia. The only personal story I ever heard (from aunts and uncles) was that he was lost from his unit in Africa, and when he returned, they told him that his mother had died back home.

My father was close to his mother, and it comes out in one of two war letters I have tucked away. The letters were given to me by an aunt, my father's sister-in-law. One was written from England, the February before the invasion. He wrote it sitting next to a generator used to supply lights. "I can hardly think for the noise," he said. The handwriting shows a man with good grammar and spelling ("furlough" is spelled correctly, and he never says "to" when he means "too"), but one who did not use periods to end sentences. In the second letter, he is writing to console a friend on the death of her husband. He tells her she has to "hold up," as he has since the death of his mother. He proves sensitive and articulate beyond what I would have expected of a farm boy from eastern North Carolina.

Sensitivity had its price, it seems. First there was the hospital after the war, and my mother says that when she met my father in 1947 he was drinking a quart of whiskey a day. He worked his job at the service station in spite of his drinking. His brothers later told me that no one ever remembers seeing him unable to function because of drinking. He was a quiet, functional drunk after the war.

What was digging so deep at him to force the shadows of war to be darkened even more by alcohol? I am not a drinker. Two beers is the outer limit of my capacity. Whatever demons I inherited from my father, demon rum is not one of them. "How can a man drink a quart of whiskey a day?" I once asked a writer I knew had been a drinker.

"It's easy. You get up in the morning and you bubble about eight ounces," the writer explained. "And then you sneak off mid-morning and you bubble about five more. Then at lunch you bubble eight more, and then mid-afternoon some more. When your shift's over you can go home and start the serious drinking until you pass out."

My father had grown up a farmer's boy tied to place, and when he left the army I'm told he tried to come home, to put in a crop of tobacco on his own. He was one of the youngest of six sons, and so maybe the farm was something to escape from. I know he left and ended up in Southern Pines, a town a hundred miles inland on U.S. Highway 1, the north-south route from New York to Florida in the days before interstates.

Some summers, when I visited my father's family, I worked in their fields, cropping tobacco or bucking hay. It was not work I enjoyed, though now, looking back, it is work I'm glad I had the privilege to do. The idea of farm, Wendell Berry reminds us, originally included the idea of household.

Maybe, one friend has suggested, it was simply that my father was good with cars. Maybe that's why he opened a gas station. "Maybe he wasn't good with farms," my friend laughed as I told him my theories of my father's flight to Southern Pines.

Southern Pines is where he met my mother, who had come north with her young daughter (my half sister) after being abandoned by a soldier in Spartanburg. My mother's father was from a farm near Southern Pines. It was what Bob Dylan would call "a simple twist of fate" that placed my mother and father—two tortured souls from different worlds—so close together after the war. I do know that he had ten good years before the bypass closed him down. Maybe it's just that he didn't see the future approaching—interstates, his own demons, and the death of the slow life. It was getting cool in central North Carolina where my father died. He had put his garden to bed for the season by the time he wandered out in the yard, got in the cold car, and took his life. Maybe a mess or two of collards survived in his garden plot, but most of his vegetables had played out over September and October. In Southern Pines, there had not been a frost by mid-November. "Killing frost," the farmers call the first frost.

I'm a collector of artifacts. My house is full of papers, books, rocks, stones, fallen leaves, bones, and pictures. I bank the past against the present the way farmers used to bank the autumn leaves against a house's foundation to protect from the winter cold.

Three decades after my father died I was in Southern Pines visiting two of my cousins. Judy, the youngest daughter of my father's brother Julian, went into a back room, brought out a yellowed newspaper. She explained how she collects old patterns and had been at a yard sale checking for dress patterns in a box. The bottom of the box was lined with old newspapers, and at the bottom of one box she had discovered this one. "It was staring up at me. I couldn't miss it." She unfolded the paper and pointed out a small news story of her uncle's suicide. "Violence Centers on Moore" the headline read. She shook her head, said, "You should have it."

This year, the newspaper is forty years old. The yellowed columns of the newspaper relate a brief narrative of my father's death. The anonymous writer explains how my father was found dead the day before, Saturday, November 15th, around 5:15 A.M. in the driveway of his home. "The windows were closed and a vacuum cleaner tube connected with the exhaust pipe had been placed in the car." There, in the next paragraph, is the name of my mother, who had found him. "She told the coroner that her husband had gone to bed at the usual time and she did not know when he'd gotten up." My sister Sandy's name and my childhood name, Johnny, appear among the survivors.

That Saturday was a day of death: the paper reports a plane had plunged into the Gulf of Mexico, killing all forty-two aboard. The whole state of Kansas was mobilized in a manhunt for the "shotgun killers" of a wealthy farmer, his wife, and two teenage children—the murders that would become the basis of *In Cold Blood.* In the brief story reporting my father's suicide, the paper also disclosed the death of a baby from accidental poisoning and another child struck and killed on a highway. There was also local news: hog prices in Raleigh, the 117th birthday of the last surviving veteran of the Civil War, girls vying for the title of "Miss Yuletide."

On my mantel is my favorite picture of my father. He is smiling, a head-and-shoulder shot. It is cold, and he wears a field jacket and helmet liner. It is taken somewhere in Europe during the Second World War. 1942 or '43. The liner sits at an angle, and a shadow falls like a woolen hat across his upper forehead. One day, I noticed something as simple as my father's teeth. They were sharp and a little crooked, not at all like my own. I searched the surface of the photograph for some clue to his suicide, his past, and the way my father's life would exert itself upon the flow of my own. What would my father look like with a beard, one such as his son has worn since his first years in college?

I found my father's last watch curled and quiet in a top drawer where my mother keeps her insurance papers. It hasn't run in years, a cheap, square-faced Timex with a brittle leather band. Sometimes, I take it out of my desk and wonder when it stopped ticking and why it wasn't buried with him. I asked my mother, and she explained how my father hated to wear a watch, a trait I've inherited. His wallet is in the drawer with his watch. Once, I took out his driver's license. Looking closely, I realized for the first time that my father was five-six. I am six-two. This discovery was a shock to me. A son always imagines his father as bigger than he is. In my father's wallet I discovered that my father was a tiny man. Physically, I'm a different man. What patterns set themselves in motion as we age, as we see our fathers more and more in the mirror looking back at us?

As November approaches I close the vents under the house, change the filter in the furnace. I mulch the slowing vegetable beds with compost and plant a last crop of lettuce and collards. I note in my journal when the hosta out front turns yellow and collapses in the cooling South Carolina nights. I work more on poems and less in the yard.

In the sequence of fourteen poems where my dead father comes to visit I challenge him with situations I imagine he would not recognize. In the poems I take my dead father's ghost to a movie, a video-poker parlor, to the beach. Each time he surprises me. He was a man who chose to leave the world of a family farm—a world that had not changed much in two hundred years—first for a war, and then for some sort of dream of a life I'll never know.

The unfinished business of these poems is mostly bickering— whether eggs are any good refrigerated, how big the garden should be, when I should change my oil, what kind of car I should drive, where we should go on vacation. My father, as he appears to me in the poems, is a difficult man, and I an unruly, disappointing son. "The dead are more with us than the living," Jacques Lacan wrote. Lacan must have known my father whose presence persists like a slow-moving cold front from beyond the grave.

When he was alive it seemed my father knew a great deal about adaptability. He left the family farm, went to war, married, had a child, ran two or three businesses. In death he is not happy with my changes. I am a man who chose to leave manual labor behind for the fluency of words and books, a choice he does not seem, through the creation of my poetic persona, to understand. I wonder what my father would make of my working this essay the way he worked his father's fields with a hoe, or completed a valve job with his socket wrenches.

I can't imagine how it must have felt, the nothingness of morning when my mother wandered out of sleep to find my father gone from bed and sensed the terrible idling engine in the dark driveway. The last huge sunflower heads nodding in the November cold. The fogged windows. The knowledge that he was gone, finally. He had tried it before, with razor blades. This time there was a deliberateness, a certainty that endures through time to this day. It was my inheritance of autumn, a pattern from birth.

By November, my father's last garden was plowed under and ready for winter. If I dropped dead tomorrow, I would leave no will behind, only sunflowers, and a poorly weeded garden already turning yellow in the autumn cold. Unlike my father, I am lazy in the rituals of civic life. I pay my bills late. I might vote as soon as not. My possessions—some property, thousands of books, clothes, furniture, a truck—would be divided up somehow. I would hope my sister would deal with it all. My mother has seen enough tragedy for one lifetime. My father's legacy to me is what is never beyond me, the idea that life could end as it began, in sudden certainty, surprising as a spark. I wish I had inherited something more useful from my father, say, his knack for growing things. It seems a connection to earth and its weather is harder to pass along than this seasonal melancholy.

Some sons are given the inheritance of summer, and for those there is a sense of full bloom, lives of fulfilled promise. These sons are the bright souls who are never alone. Others are born into the hint of infinite possibility, of bloom, with spring emerging in every moment. Others, it seems, walk into life already in deep cold.

My father died in November because he was winter's child, and he could not see his way through another one. Maybe that's explanation enough. My birth and his death made me autumn's child. With his suicide he gave me the month of November with its warm days and cool nights.

This year I mark his final passing with a last harvest, this essay, the fruit of my father's vine.

HILLS LIKE
WHITE HILLS

W. D. WETHERELL

ANYTHING HIGH MIGHT HAVE TAKEN HIS SON. TRANSMISSION
lines, a radio tower, trees. Crows even, migrating geese, though it had
been late in the year for geese. Ordinary phone lines for that matter,
a church steeple, a bullet sent skyward by a disappointed hunter or
bored kid. Something high had taken him, and so over the course of
the year Anderson had become adept at driving with his eyes near
the ground. Pavement, shoulders, roadside grass. This was the flat,
expansive safety his son never found, and it seemed that if he concentrated on it steadily enough, kept himself from glancing higher, things
might be reversed.

It was harder in these hills. Almost certainly it had been a hill that
had done the killing. They rose above the road, pinching in the highway, waiting every time his eyes moved toward the shaded part of
the windshield with its matching crescents of frost. Two days before
Christmas, this early in the morning, there weren't many cars, yet ne-
gotiating the curves required him to look up and look up often, his
own safety at stake. Safety? It made him smile, thinking in those terms.

"Mission" was the better word. He had one last mission left to per-
form, and then he would be done with safety as a notion that ever
need concern him again.

The hills became higher and whiter once he turned north onto the
secondary road marked on the directions. He remembered twenty
years before bringing Tom up to camp through similar hills, and how
they had played the game of trying to make each mountain into a familiar shape. A llama, a roller coaster, an elephant. He remembered—

and felt not the sadness he might have expected, but a weary kind of disgust. Good times to mock the bad ones, life's easy and bitter trick. The hills that confronted him out the windshield refused to be anything but stark white hills, and the deeper he drove into them, the more their literalness seemed to matter, matter hard.

The search had come west, but not this far. Those in charge had drawn compass lines every direction from the airport a distance of sixty miles; where those lines intersected hills above twenty-five hundred feet the lines had stopped. The hills on his right were that high and more—an insurmountable barrier, according to the experts. No one, flying in the fog they had experienced last Christmas Eve, could hope to get past them. The search had been inside the tighter circle, but the search found nothing, the leaves had come back on the trees and then dropped again, hunting season had gone by without anyone spotting anything, and the snow had the woods for a second winter, blotting out with its whiteness the whiteness of the plane.

And now this man, this Mr. Ayers, with his telephone message and letter, the carefully penciled directions to his store. A woman he knew had heard a plane Christmas Eve low in the hills. Another person in town, an ice fisherman, had seen a flash in the trees, and if you drew a line west from the airport into Vermont there was a gap through the hills it might just be possible for a plane to have entered before the hills joined ridges and closed back in.

Anderson knew it was a slim hope at best, but this was what he was down to as the anniversary date drew near—following through on every sighting, every rumor, every vague impulse his son's plane had left in people's wondering. If he worried about Mr. Ayers it wasn't about his being wrong, but about his being a crank. So far he had managed to avoid these, the ones who divined Tom's whereabouts through astrology or dowsing rods or home computers. It would have been intolerable, meeting any of these, listening to them babble on.

Mr. Ayers, from their brief conversation, did not seem like a crank. So it was worth the long drive north, meeting him, listening to his theory, trying once again to find closure. It was the word everyone used in justifying the time and expense that had gone into the search... We need a finish to this, the state police said, the fish and game people, the aviation experts sent by the government. We need closure... and he'd heard the word so many times, pronounced it so often in various appeals of his own, it seemed to have become part of him, a stencil over his heart. When he imagined his son's final seconds it was always the rushing vertigo, the blinding forwardness, the shoulder straps tightening, straining, snapping—but try as he would, summon up all of his courage, he could never get past that moment, imagine impact, not unless he knew for certain where that impact happened.

At first the country had been familiar to him from fishing trips, foliage drives when Alice was alive and they had gone north for long weekends, but this changed at the next turn in the directions, and he drove through a leaner, sparer kind of land, the hills leaving only a narrow strip into which were pressed a river, the road, a few scattered farms. All were abandoned, their yards empty and scraped clean— survivors of everything the century had thrown at them, only to succumb here in its last few seconds to forces he could only guess at. The houses came a little thicker as he neared the village. Fifties style most of them, erected back in the days when everyone dreamed of the suburban life, weathering horribly now, beyond rescue by paint or carpentry or TLC. Most had some attempts at decoration—a plastic wreath, a string of lights—but they looked like neglected leftovers from previous years, and it made it seem as though Christmas were a much darker kind of celebration here, something that spoke of sternness and not joy. But it suited him. The grayness, the flinty farms, the sagging lights. Suited him and cradled him in.

The last turn mentioned in the directions came at a rectangular green sign, Ayers Store 3 Miles. Almost immediately he passed an obstacle he hadn't thought about before, a rusty steel windmill poking well above the ridgeline, dark vines twisted all the way to the top. He winced, brought his head down, felt again the rushing sensation in his chest. The village, when he arrived, was a grouping of six or seven old houses around the white patch of a common that sloped downhill, with the store and its gas pumps set against the higher end, a small yellow church against the lower.

The store itself was as old as any of the houses; asphalt shingles covered the sides, but the pumps and sign looked new, suggesting a recent infusion of energy and cash. Anderson had no illusions about the current state of country stores, and so the inside was pretty much as he expected. The salty things in one row, the sugary things in the other; the beer in a cooler along the back wall, pornography in a rack to the other side; the lottery tickets there by the register with the nicotine. A stout man wearing an apron was ringing up a customer, and so Anderson waited his turn, standing by the shelf with the candy Kisses and M&M's, all done up in holiday packaging, so it was by far the brightest corner in the store.

"Mr. Ayers?" he said, when the customer had gone. "I'm Tom Anderson. Tom Senior."

There was a pause long and surprised enough for Anderson to worry he had made a mistake, and then the man smiled, nodded, rubbed his hands down his apron, and stuck one out.

"An honor, sir. A real honor and pleasure."

He was a man in his early fifties, with the kind of stocky good health that made Anderson think of a butcher from the old neighborhood, with the same square and delicate hands. His first surprise mastered, he pulled his apron off, went over to the door, put the Closed sign up, then came back, the eagerness having burst from his eyes over the rest of his face, making it shine.

"Coffee? Yeah, me too. Didn't think you'd come, you know, when we talked and all. But it's like you said there on TV. You were willing to follow the slightest lead, and so that's why I wrote that letter, got in touch."

There was a lot of New York in his voice, the inflection and speed. "The city?" he said, when Anderson asked him about it. "Oh yeah, way back when some. Up here they thought I was a rapist or something when we first moved in. Now? Vermont all the way. Snowmobiles, ATVs, skiing. Hey, this is kid stuff. Lived in Alaska for a winter, worked on the pipeline saving up money for a place like this. But that's what got me when I saw you talking about how your son wanted to be a bush pilot in Alaska someday, how that's what he was working toward. I could relate to that right off the bat."

Anderson was used to this now, the eager way people approached the puzzle of his son's loss. There was a time when it seemed everyone was looking for the plane, then a time when no one was, and now a small hard-core group had taken over, the police scanner boys, the ones who always kept rescue gear loaded in the back of their trucks. It was another reason he had come north again—to head them off, throw a solution at them before things got out of hand. He didn't want Tom's disappearance to go into the next stage, become an unsolved mystery, written up in anniversary articles when the rest of the news was thin, the fodder for hacks. Literalness was what he wanted, answers. Hills like white hills. Death like sudden death.

Ayers kept talking as they walked out to his pickup. Ice coated the windshield, and by the time the defroster got going they were already pulling over to the side of the road. It was an overlook, a wide one. Below them the river wound like a flat shoelace between dark pockets of pine, but in every other direction the terrain was high and blocky looking, the hills so tightly merged it was as if they'd been towed there and dumped.

Ayers slapped his hand on the dashboard, then turned sideways in the seat. "Just want to get my facts straight, follow my train of reasoning. Sound good?"

"Sounds good," Anderson said.

"Your son was in a hurry, right? I mean no offense, but he was in a hurry. Rented a car to drive to New Hampshire where he was assigned to take a Lear jet home for this rich guy, right? A ferry job, straight and simple. But it's Christmas Eve, right? A foggy day, not so hot for flying, but he's young, he's just started on the job, and he's crazy about Lears." He hesitated, reached over for the coffee. "A girlfriend, right?"

"Fiancée. Her name is Jennifer."

"Right. So he's in a hurry on account of that, too. He doesn't fly any way like all those morons from the FAA think. Doesn't follow the river or the interstate or anything obvious. He's really sure of himself, a pilot who knows he's good. So he takes a shortcut across the hills . . . Okay, that's nearly impossible it was so foggy, even flying on instruments. But there's a gap, you look at the map and there's a gap. Maybe he knows about it and maybe he doesn't, but that gap is five miles east of here, and it leads to only one place." He tapped his knuckles against the windshield. "There. Those mountains out there. They go a thousand feet up in the course of two ridges. Looming up at him like a wall, a complete dead end."

Anderson listened carefully, keeping his hands around his own coffee, very aware of how prim and weak they must look there, cup and hands, motionless on his knee.

"You said on the phone a man had seen something," he said, with less impatience in his tone than he actually felt.

Ayers turned back from the window and nodded. "Bernie Beliveau. He was out ice fishing on Sanderson Pond. Right about…" He leaned forward. "Down there. A little deaf, Bernie is, but there's nothing wrong with his seeing. He noticed a flash, something bright enough to make his eyes blink. This would have been two-thirty or so—he didn't have a watch. But it squares with the flight time and all."

"Has anyone checked it out?"

"Sure. Snowmobile club. They haven't found anything, not yet. The ice was pretty thin in some spots. Could have gone right through down to the bottom."

"Can I talk to him?"

"He's out of town. Quebec, his wife's family for Christmas. Jesus, wouldn't you know it. Just when you arrive."

"There's also this woman you spoke of. The one who heard something."

Ayers nodded, vigorously this time. "Sarah Hall. Yeah, that's what I was going to do actually. Drive us out there so you can hear for yourself."

He backed them up, skidded on the snow, then turned down a dirt road that sloped toward the river. It was a short drive—just long enough for Ayers to go over the basics. Sarah was a great old gal, he said. Almost eighty-six now and sharp as a tack. A tough life of course. Born when the hills were emptying out, little money around, meager prospects, not much hope. Lived with her parents long past being a girl, having the care of them when they got sick, running the farm alone. Parents dying just after VJ day, then she got polio, so she wasn't any freer than before. One brother, a bum. Niece she loved, took care of, but then the niece went bad, too, moved west with a slick, handsome liar, broke Sarah's heart. Lived alone now, helped by a friend or two from the church. The last of her kind really. Last one wedded so tightly to the hills.

"My wife Janet's gotten to know her better than me," Ayers said, both hands on the wheel now, the road turning bumpy. "She's a visiting nurse, so she comes out here once a week minimum. She's the one heard the story about what happened Christmas Eve. It's a little vague, but I think there's something to it. She's not crazy or anything, even living alone for so long. She never makes anything up."

Was this meant to reassure him? Anderson nodded, trying not to let his skepticism show. He had learned a long time ago that hope had nothing to do with his mission, which was to follow every thread, every possible lead, until it gave out. And that's what he pictured strung along the road ahead of them—a gray, all but invisible thread, in tatters, separating, so when they bounced over a narrow log bridge, turned left on a one-lane road under a hoop of bare trees, it was as if they were following the wispiest corner of the wispiest end of the wispiest strand hope ever spun.

They stopped and got out beside an old Cape farmhouse that was easily two hundred years old. It had no charm, nor quaintness. Adjoining it, connected, was a barn that had collapsed long enough ago that a large maple grew out of the wreckage. The house seemed on its way to collapsing as well—the roof was moss covered, hardly distinct from the grassy bluff its eaves almost touched, and where the peak should be was a mushy sag of rotted shingles.

Ayers tried the door, peered into its window. Behind the house was a large field, the uncut hay sticking up through the snow in slender, flesh-colored bristles. It was flat enough to land a plane on—Anderson recognized this immediately. But the pilot would have had to be extraordinarily lucky or extraordinarily skilled, because where the field ended, with no intermission, rose a hill, high and abrupt enough it blotted out the sun.

"Don't hear anyone," Ayers said, waving him over. "Let's just go in."

It took a few minutes for Anderson's eyes to grow used to the dark. Inside the door was a hall decorated with sentimental old paintings in rough-hewn frames, the kind itinerant painters had once turned out for a night's room and board. Adjoining this was a neatly furnished parlor, dominated by a woodstove so ornate it looked Arabian, and past this a kind of enclosed porch, which by some magic of positioning had gathered unto itself, like a prism, what sunlight managed to filter down from the clouds. The furniture was plainer here, a deacon's bench and maple rocker, and there was a regular gallery of snapshots taped to the wall, pictures of animals, farms, and fairs, the most recent of which seemed to have been taken fifty years before.

It was what was in the center of the room that surprised him most: a Christmas tree, and not a small one, reaching all the way to the ceiling, decorated with paper chains and heavy-looking tinsel. It was fresh enough that the spruce smell was strong and bracing, yet not so overpowering it could hide another smell he had caught when he first came in. Almond or almond extract, a warm smell, the kind that came with baking.

Ayers tiptoed and peered like he expected to find her dead. "Miss Hall? It's Don Ayers. Janet's husband? You know, from the store?"

No one answered. Ayers had turned to go back into the parlor when Anderson put his hand on his arm and tilted his head toward the one corner the tree did not completely hide. Sitting there in an old wicker wheelchair was a woman who seemed, in that first glance, little more than a forgotten gathering of wrinkles, with eyes that floated above the collection and calmly regarded it, brought it to life.

Ayers put his hand over his heart. "There you are!"

He went over to the window, pushed the shades up, let in more light. Anderson could see her quite plainly now. Her legs were covered by a plaid wool throw, and her chest was hidden by pillows she clutched as a child would stuffed animals, yet somehow he got the impression of great strength, or at least strength's shadow. Again, this came mostly from her eyes, which regarded them both the same calm, even way they regarded her own frailty. She moved them from Ayers's face to Anderson's, lingered there, then brought her hand up to locate her forehead, take a girlish swipe at a last trace of white hair.

"Yes, come in," she said, or something like that.

Anderson, wondering how to approach her, took his cue from the house itself, the air of quiet that had been bundled up and secreted away, but Ayers didn't sense this and squatted down beside her wheelchair talking far too loudly.

"This is Mr. Anderson come up here all the way from the city just to talk to you. He's lost his son, in an accident. I want you to tell him what you told Janet, just the same way."

"Crows," she said, or something like that. "Watching them, looking for corn out on the meadow before you came. No corn there in thirty years. Joke on them."

"Last Christmas Eve," Ayers said, obviously not understanding a word. "You know, the story you told Janet about what happened Christmas Eve."

She smiled, like she had him. "Christmas Eve is tomorrow."

"Last Christmas Eve. What happened then."

Too abrupt of him, not the way it was done, a story on demand for visitors who had likely not eaten. Her reaction was plain enough. She tried to get up, move toward the almond smell, but the blanket was too heavy, and she settled back into the chair with a disdainful, impotent wave of her hand. When she started her story it seemed out of frustration more than anything—that being so weak there was no power open to her other than what she could generate with words.

It was hard understanding her, the odd cadence of her voice. It wasn't just the old hill-country accent, the dividing up of syllables, but the way she blended the end of one word into the beginning of the next—musically, but a music that had been played so often, for so many years, it had lost all variation in pitch, came out as the kind of hoarse, undifferentiated sound a piano would make if all the keys were pressed at once. The deeper she got into her story the harder Anderson stared trying to concentrate, catching up with her only in the pauses, translating to himself before looking over toward Ayers and translating out loud.

It had been a miserable Christmas Eve. Snow fog, ground wet, the air too warm for December. Remembered feeling blue herself. The field behind the barn, going out to let the cows in from the river. Dumb old cows. Good for nothing old cows. She'd taken to hating them, only creatures she saw most days, no one coming anymore to visit. Leaving the radio back on in the house, loud as possible, gave her some company. Lying awake at night listening to the trains heading south, wishing she were going that way herself. That lonely rumble it put in the air. Nice sound. Thing of the past. Billy Sykes worked on the railroad. His mother was cousin to her mother, though they never saw either one of them after the fire.

Anderson listened, managed to stay with her even in the tangents, but only with great effort. He stared at the firm line of her lips, the one place the wrinkles successfully fought back, trying to get help from the way they shaped and decorated each word. Old age had always been something remote to him, a land glimpsed from a safe distance, but he was close enough now it concerned him intensely, the hoarse croaking it put into a voice, the way even simple stories had to flutter back and forth before emerging. He must learn all this, prepare himself, before he was tossed beaten and ragged on the same hard shore.

"Fast for you?" she asked, aware now of his attention, anxious to keep it. He shook his head, waited for her to go on.

It was about two or so, past lunchtime, when she stopped and looked up. It wasn't a sound, not at first, so much as a slight wavery pressure on the back of her neck. What's this? she wondered, turning around. Still nothing. But then up way back of Job's Hill there was a raspy coughing sound like the generator made just before conking out. She bent her head back, shaded her eyes to peer. It didn't bore in or race away like most sounds did that reached the farm, but looped around in a tight circle, echoing, like the hills were playing a game with whatever the sound came from, tossing it back and forth just for fun.

She knew right exactly what it was. Airplane. She'd heard airplanes before. At the fairs and then once in the city where she'd taken her mother when she first got sick. Knew it was in trouble, too. She couldn't see anything because of the fog, but she could hear real clear. Kind of a snapping, sputtering sound, but weak and troubled, so she wanted to put her hands under it somehow, boost it back up over the hills to where it belonged.

Anderson was so engrossed in isolating the words that he didn't pay much attention to the thrust of what she was saying, not at first. He trusted Ayers to pay attention for both of them, but Ayers was shaking his head now, frowning in confusion.

"What year was this, Miss Hall?"

She pulled down on the corner of her mouth, stared off toward the Christmas tree, widened her eyes.

"Cows," Ayers said, glancing over at him. "Come on. When was the last time they had cows here?"

"My parents were away," Sarah said, with a look that managed to be coy and beseeching at the same time, as if she knew a secret and wanted help getting it out.

"What year, Miss Hall?"

"Roosevelt year."

"Roosevelt?"

"Whipped Hoover. Whipped him good. Father cried."

Ayers put his hand against his forehead. "Oh my sweet Jesus," he whispered. "Nineteen goddam thirty-two."

Anderson had seen that look too many times not to recognize it instantly. On state police captains putting down the telephone with a grimace of disappointment, pilots getting out from their search planes, shrugging, turning their thumbs down, volunteers slogging back out of the woods exhausted after another long day with no trace. The look of hope hitting a wall. He was surprised at how disappointed he felt himself, having been so careful. Grasping at threads and here he was grasping one all right, the withered rotten end.

Ayers, not daring to meet Anderson's eyes, went over to the wheelchair and knelt down. "Thank you for your time, Miss Hall. Janet will look in on you tonight, that's what she told me. You want anything from the store you call, and I'll see she brings it. You have yourself a nice Christmas, okay?"

Sarah fussed the blanket closer up her chin, looked over at Anderson with a peculiar kind of curiosity—making an appeal, though he had no idea what it could be for. Mumbling his own thanks, doing his best to smile for her, he followed Ayers back outside to the truck.

Neither one said anything at first. The truck bounced off the dirt onto pavement, and it was only the heavy jolt of it that made talk possible.

"I'm sorry, Mr. Anderson," Ayers said. "I should have gone out and checked on the story myself. Hey, it sounded good, what I heard from my wife. She's pretty sharp, you'll agree on that."

And Anderson was used to this, too, comforting people who had tried comforting him. "That's all right. No, I enjoyed meeting her. It wasn't your fault."

He knew them too well, what words he should mumble. Always before they had been sincere, but whether because of being tired after the long drive or the anniversary rolling around in another day, he felt irritated with Ayers, anxious to be done with him, and it took a real effort to keep this from infecting his tone.

He came into the store before leaving. Ayers was off on a new tack, promising to have Beliveau call him when he got back, talking about organizing a search party once the holidays were over. He pressed a list of telephone numbers into Anderson's coat pocket, insisted they stay in touch. Anderson bought a coffee for the drive, hesitated, then went to the shelf with candy and bought a box of marzipan fruit, the most elaborately decorated box in the store.

He'd been daydreaming earlier, not paying attention, but the tread marks left by Ayers's truck were still easy to make out in the snow. He parked by the collapsed barn, followed their footprints, knocked on the door, and went in. As before, he was struck by the almond scent, the warmth of baking, and this time he investigated, searching the small box of a kitchen for its source. There was a blackened teapot on the stove, a saucepan of water, but the oven below it was cold and lifeless. Even the counter, the old maple cutting boards—they were smooth and clean, with no dusting of flour. Whatever was wafting to him had its origin in the past, a memory of Christmas so remote he couldn't locate it for certain, and it amazed him, to think something so forgotten could still be so strong.

He went in toward the parlor, expecting to find her still in her wheelchair. She must have heard his car, because she was up now, walking in from the sunroom, her right leg dragging behind her in a separate, jerkier rhythm, but otherwise moving with surprising litheness and strength. She nodded, seeing him. "Knew it," she mumbled, or something like that, then waved him with a little curtsying motion over toward the couch.

"This is for you," he said.

She took the package, smiled politely, then smiled for real, her hands going down to fumble with the wrapping until she had it apart. A greedy child—that's what he thought of—or maybe a child who wasn't used to presents, and so couldn't help herself from tearing right in. She unhinged the box, held it up to her face to peek inside, put two fingers in, pulled out a marzipan cherry, held it up to the light.

"For you," he said, again. She shook her head, held the candy up to her mouth, made a gumming kind of motion. Not without teeth— she pantomimed this perfectly. It was his turn to smile now, but she must have been concerned about hurting his feelings, because she very daintily took each candy out from its compartment and lined them up on the windowsill—pink apple, yellow peach, pink banana, their color brightening the entire room.

When she came back she sat beside him on the sofa, sank in just far enough that her shoulder came against his and nestled to a stop. On the end table were some religious pamphlets, and she handed him one—whether as a gift of her own or because of his loss, he wasn't sure. He regarded it for a decent few minutes, turned a few pages, closed it again, then pointed behind them toward the window.

"What happened next?"

He was sure no one had ever asked her that before, to finish a story. She smiled like he'd given her another gift, one she could take her time with. Oh, that's a wonderful story, she said, in the same blur of syllables. Whether it was because he was alone with her now or because he'd grown used to their rhythm, the words seemed much clearer this time, and he had no trouble keeping up. For a while she had thought the sound was gone, and she felt sad about that, without knowing why. But it came back again, just as she was turning toward the house to finish her chores. This time it was so loud she covered up her ears, like a motorcycle was racing toward her from the sky. It's going to crash—she was sure of this—but then the air suddenly went softer, and she spun around and around trying to locate the feathery little whisper that had taken the roar's place.

She saw it now, back on the far side of the field and maybe a hundred feet above it, dropping as smoothly and uniformly as could be imagined, so it was less like an airplane landing on the meadow than it was the meadow going up to meet the airplane. There's too much snow, she decided, suddenly alarmed, but then the wheels were kicking through the crust, sending up a wake that crested over the wings and dusted them in powder... the motor came on again and deepened, the black propeller spun madly and slowed... and then the plane was landing on the far end of the field near the apple trees, skidding around and starting back, coming to a stop not ten yards from where she stood watching, clutching her hat.

A little two-seater, smaller even than the planes she had seen at fairs. The fabric on the wings was painted yellow, stretched so tight it glistened even in the grayness, and there was a big number seven painted on the tail in scarlet-colored dope that still looked wet. The nose rose much higher than the tail, so it was hard to see anything more than this, but then from the rear seat there was a smooth kind of lifting motion, a leather cap emerging, then a leather jacket, then an actual shape, boosting itself free of the seat's skirted rim, jumping out onto the wing, vaulting down.

"Whew!" the pilot said, wiping his hand in an exaggerated gesture across his forehead. He pointed toward the steep hill at the end of the field, tugged his cap off, and laughed.

She knew at once he was the handsomest man she had ever seen, or handsomest boy. He was her age—she knew that, too, right down to the year and season, or how else to explain the instinctive sympathy she felt at once? Between the blond hair that blew down from his cap, the easy good humor of his expression, his flawless, suntanned skin, he was exactly what you would expect to emerge from such a machine. What's more, he seemed to know this, seemed to take an active, innocent pleasure in being so perfectly wedded to the power and grace he controlled.

"What's your name?" he asked, tilting his head as if to see right past her shyness, put all that aside.

She told him and he nodded. "Well, Sarah, that little mountain of yours almost did it for me. A close shave! Great fun, did you hear me gunning it?" He followed her eyes. "Curtis Scout, a beauty. An old one, war surplus, but I fixed it up brand-new. Flying the mail, started yesterday. Burlington to Boston and I thought I knew the shortcuts, but looks like I thought wrong... You're an awfully pretty girl, know that? No, I guess you don't. Not living out here you wouldn't. I guess I've got to be going, what a shame."

Her face burned with this, what he was telling her, but she met his look without turning away, feeling as if something very important rested on doing this. The pilot pulled his cap on, pushed his cowlick to tuck it under, started toward the wing, then suddenly turned back to her and smiled.

"Ever been up?"

She shook her head.

"Want to?"

She shook her head again.

"Aw, come on. It doesn't hurt. It's clearing up now, you'll be amazed at what it's like."

She didn't know which meant more to her, staring at the plane or staring at him, but that didn't matter because it was all the same, pilot and airplane, and he must have sensed this in her, knew all along what she was going to say. His words caused a lifting sensation through her entire body, a warmth surging up from her toes toward her waist, and it was no use struggling, though she did one last time.

"Too many hills," she said softly, teasing him, marveling at being able to tease.

The pilot glanced over the field and squinted. "That puny little thing? Hills thrills! Here, I've got some extra duds in the cockpit. You can sit in front. Up ten minutes, some quick sightseeing, then I'll bring you down again, I promise."

He cupped his hands together, boosted her up onto the wing. Inside the cockpit was a leather flying jacket like the one he wore, only newer, and he held it for her while she put it on, then handed her some goggles that turned everything amber. The cockpit itself was small and tight as a glove, though open on top. He showed her how to fasten the shoulder belts, told her to make sure to grab hold of the bar on the side if he did any fancy stuff, then—after looking at her carefully, breaking into his widest grin yet—scooted around behind her and lowered himself down into the pilot's seat a foot or so behind hers.

"Let me know if you get scared!" he shouted, and then everything became lost in the sudden roar of the engine, the propeller's kick, reversal, and whirr, the clean, light smell of camphor that streamed back from the pistons and made her dizzy.

He bumped the plane out to the middle of the field, gunned the engine, started out. She had never gone this fast on land before, let alone the sky, and the speed pressed against her breasts, making her even giddier than the camphor, even more than the rush of stone walls and hemlocks that seemed suddenly to have become liquid. Too fast, she decided, wanting to scream and laugh both, and then the motion slowed and vanished, the pressure moved off her breasts toward her shoulders, and she realized with an overpowering sensation of delight that what she had heard about, read about, seen in the distance was actually true—that they were airborne, in the air, flying.

She didn't have time to be scared, though she should have been. He'd taken off away from the steepest hill, but there were plenty of hills in this direction, too. She couldn't see any, not with the haze, but he must have—either that or maybe he didn't care a fig for things like mountains and ridges, thumbed his nose at them, trusted to luck. They banked around and around and ever upward until between one moment and the next they were at the top edge of the mist, the last wet tatters streaming against the fuselage, the propeller whirring free of it into sunshine, into a world that had been above her every livelong day of her life, but that she had no conception of, not until now.

They were above the clouds, above every hill and mountain, so there was nothing to be seen except endless white beneath them, endless blue straight above. Never had she dreamed of such flatness and expanse. She knew the word "horizontal," had learned it in school, but she realized now there had been nothing in her world to demonstrate that property, not when compared to this. Endless—every which way was endless, without walls. As they turned into the sun she had to shut her eyes, even under the goggles, the gold flaring out the white and blue, shredding them into ribbons. Behind her the pilot was banging on the fuselage, shouting something she couldn't hear. Hold on? She was already holding on, she couldn't hold on tighter, never in her life had she held anything so tight, the pressure moving back on her chest again as he gunned the plane straight up toward the sun.

Just when it seemed the wings must break off from their throbbing, the plane leveled off—leveled off just long enough for her to feel on the back of her neck above the flying jacket a sensation that was cool and warm both, as if someone had kissed her. A second later she heard a happy laugh, even above the motor—a laugh and so she knew it had been a kiss after all. The plane tipped over into a dive, powering right back toward the clouds it had with such effort escaped, touching the grayness, dipping into it like a kingfisher dipping into a pond, boring the happiness deep inside where no one could ever steal it out, then looping back up again to start the whole process over—the momentary leveling, the tender kiss on the back of her neck, the laugh, and then the diving back to the soft edge of clouds.

Four times he did this, five, and then six. Forever! is what she wanted to shout, but on the seventh dive he kept the plane plunging down into the dampness. The motor began sputtering, they banked steeply to avoid something she couldn't see, banked a second time, then broke free into the transparent gray below the opaque layer... came level over the field... coasted, skipped once, set down.

She was shy again, being down. The pilot jumped out of his seat and stripped off his goggles, then balanced his way over to help her onto the wing.

"That high enough for you? That's flying, Miss Sarah Hall. That's flying and you did fine."

It was strange, those next few minutes. He had been so dashing and confident before, but now he seemed sadder, being on the ground, standing next to her, neither one of them knowing what to say. He looked over toward the house, up toward the sky, then directly at her—seemed trying to connect them all somehow, not sure how to go about it.

"I suppose you have lots of company, it being Christmas."

No, she told him. She wanted to laugh at his thinking that. Her mother and father were in town, and she was alone.

The pilot stared at her, seemed trying to reach a decision. "Alone, huh? Oh boy. Nice warm fireplace too, I'll bet." He looked up and winced. "Won't have much time, real clouds now, not that flimsy stuff. Mail to deliver, all these Christmas letters people are waiting for... Look, I've got to go before I get socked in solid. But I'll come back, understand that? No matter what happens, maybe sometime when you least expect it, I'll come back."

She wanted him to kiss her and not on the neck this time, but shyness still troubled them, and it wasn't until he was back in the cockpit that he seemed his laughing, exuberant self. "Thank you!" she yelled, over the motor, but she wasn't sure he heard. He taxied around to the edge of the field, following the tracks they had made in landing, then gave her a little wave before starting off, even faster and more abruptly than he had the first time, making her think of an arrow pulled back and back and back and suddenly released, to fly free through the air God knows where.

Nothing left but sound after that, the same lost echo as before. Hills had it, played with it, tossed it back and forth, let it go. Then? The snowy field at her feet with two long grooves. A bolt that had shaken loose off the plane, sharp end stuck in the crust. Standing there staring. Chores to do. Cows waiting. Dumb old stupid cows. Water to haul. Supper. Radio. Bed.

The entire time she talked the pressure of her shoulder had been against Anderson's, but now, finishing, she sat more erect and the couch separated them into a formal, stiff position it was difficult to maintain. When he got up he got up gingerly, not wanting to do anything that would cause her to tip back toward the empty half. She had her eyes closed. He walked quietly toward the door, leaving his coat on the chair as a kind of pledge. I'll come back soon.

Outside, the gray wore a purple undertone, the preliminary to blackness, and the ground was far lighter than the sky. His shoes squeaked so loud on the snow it scared up a ring of crows pecking at brown apples near the barn. Past it he came out onto the field, or at least its near edge. It was long and rectangular, and it wasn't hard to picture a plane landing, even with the saplings and birch that had possession now of its center.

He took several steps more, then turned to face the steep hill on the north side, the hill her pilot had somehow avoided. It rose much blacker than any other part of the sky, though he could still see the scraggly outline of its trees, notice how they seemed like sutures holding the steepness together. Sutures, like sutures. He stood there a long time, enough for his feet to turn cold, his shoulders to start shaking. He felt the same rushing sensation he had felt all year, the hurtling through space, and he was flying in the center of it, everything falling past him, the sky down his throat, and this time he tried closing his eyes to it, close them until they matted together in wetness, the shudder deepened, the cold and hardness entered him, turned him over, split him apart in an explosion of tree limbs, shattered him senseless on the rocks.

He opened his eyes. He ran his hands down his sides, blinked to find himself in the blackness, whatever puny stuff the rocks hadn't bothered smashing. He saw Sarah Hall coming toward him across the snow, backlit by what light streamed from the house, limping horribly, punishing herself, but moving steadily on, a wool coat around her shoulders, his own coat borne on her outstretched arms like a king's precious robe. And it wasn't her weakness that he fixed on, not the whole of her, but what she was wearing on her feet—the heavy galoshes, the kind with buckles, the boots he had worn himself as a boy.

She came up to him, let the coat slide back toward her chest, reached toward his arm with a blindness he hadn't noticed indoors, the wrinkles in her cheeks tensing and puckering as if to take the place of eyes. She found his wrist first, then his sweater, the material by the elbow, bunching it, going higher, finally tightening on the old useless muscle of his arm.

Poor man! she said—not out loud, not even in a whisper, but by direct transmission through her hand.

They turned toward the only light visible. In its decay, in its sturdiness, the house looked like an ark set on a cradle of yellow slats. Tugging him after her, helping each other over the tricky spots, they followed the openings her boots had plowed through the snow.

Kim Barnes's first memoir, *In the Wilderness*, received the PEN/Jerard Fund Award and was a finalist for the 1997 Pulitzer Prize in Biography/Autobiography. Her second memoir, *Hungry for the World*, was published by Villard–Random House. She lives with her husband and children above the Clearwater River in Idaho.

Dorothy Barresi is the author of *All of the Above* and *The Post-Rapture Diner*, which won an American Book Award. She has been the recipient of fellowships from the National Endowment for the Arts and the Fine Arts Work Center in Provincetown. Her poems have been published in numerous literary journals, and she is a regular contributor of essay-reviews to the *Gettysburg Review*. She directs the creative writing program at California State University, Northridge, and lives in Los Angeles with her husband and sons.

Rick Bass is the author of sixteen books of fiction and nonfiction, including a novel, *Where the Sea Used to Be;* an essay collection, *Brown Dog of the Yaak;* and, most recently, *Colter: The True Story of the Best Dog I Ever Had.* He lives in Montana.

Douglas Carlson's essays have appeared in such journals as *Ascent, American Literary Review,* and the *Georgia Review.* A coauthored book, *When We Say We're Home: A Quartet of Place and Memory,* was published by the University of Utah Press. Currently, he is teaching writing at Concordia College in Moorhead, Minnesota.

Katharine Coles's third collection of poetry, *The Golden Years of the Fourth Dimension,* will be published in 2001 by the University of Nevada Press, which also published her second collection, *A History of the Garden,* and her novel, *The Measurable World.* Her fiction and poetry have appeared in several anthologies and in many journals, including the *Paris Review, Prairie*

Schooner, and *Ascent.* She directs and teaches in the creative writing program at the University of Utah, where she is an associate professor of English.

Elizabeth Dodd teaches literature and creative writing at Kansas State University. Her most recent books, *Asylum and Other Essays into Place and Past* (a collection of essays) and *Archetypal Light* (a collection of poetry), are forthcoming from the University of Utah Press and the University of Nevada Press, respectively.

Diane Glancy published five books in 1999: a novel, *Fuller Man;* a collection of stories, *Moyer Bell: The Voice That Was in Travel;* a novella, *The Closets of Heaven;* a collection of poetry, *(Ado)ration;* and an anthology edited with Mark Nowak, *Visit Teepee Town: Native Writing after the Detours.* She teaches at Macalester College in St. Paul, Minnesota.

John Lane is the writer-in-residence at Wofford College in Spartanburg, South Carolina. He has published two volumes of poems and a book of essays, *Weed Time.* He has also edited three anthologies of personal essays, most recently *The Woods Stretched for Miles: New Southern Nature Writing.* He is a cofounder of the Hub City Writers Project.

Michael Martone is the author of a collection of essays, *The Flatness and Other Landscapes,* and five books of short fiction, including *Seeing Eye* and *Pensés: The Thoughts of Dan Quayle.* He has edited two collections of essays about the Midwest: *A Place of Sense: Essays in Search of the Midwest* and *Townships: Pieces of the Midwest.* He is a professor of English and directs the program in creative writing at the University of Alabama. He lives in Tuscaloosa with the poet Theresa Pappas and their two sons, Sam and Nick.

Naomi Shihab Nye lives with her husband, photographer Michael Nye, and their thirteen-year-old son, Madison, in a hundred-year-old house a block from the San Antonio River in Texas. She is the author of *Fuel, Red Suitcase,* and *Words under the Words,* collections of poetry, and *Never in a Hurry,* a collection of essays. Her most recent anthologies are *Salting the Ocean:* 100 Poems by Young Poets, and *What Have You Lost?*

Peggy Shumaker's work has appeared in the Alaskan issue of *Prairie Schooner* and in the anthologies *Looking North* and *Under Northern Lights.*

She is professor emerita at the University of Alaska–Fairbanks, where she taught creative writing for many years.

W. D. Wetherell's books include the novel *Chekhov's Sister* and the story collection *The Man Who Loved Levittown*. His new novel, *Morning*, is forthcoming from Pantheon Books. He is the current holder of the Strauss Living Award from the American Academy of Arts and Letters.

John Pedersen

W. Scott Olsen, an associate professor of English and chair of the environmental studies program at Concordia College in Moorhead, Minnesota, is the author of a story collection, two travel books, and a textbook. He edited the special essay issue of *American Literary Review,* coedited the anthology *The Sacred Place,* and currently edits the literary magazine *Ascent.* His work has been twice cited among the notable essays appearing in the *Best American Essays,* in 1997 and 1999. He is one of four contributors to and the editor of the book *When We Say We're Home: A Quartet of Place and Memory,* a collection of essays.

COURTESY OF Michael Heargerty/Villard

Bret Lott is the author of the novels *The Man Who Owned Vermont, A Stranger's House, Reed's Beach, The Hunt Club,* and the best-selling novel and Oprah's Book Club pick *Jewel.* He is also the author of the story collections *A Dream of Old Leaves* and *How to Get Home,* and the memoir *Fathers, Sons, and Brothers.* His short stories and essays have been widely anthologized, and have appeared in such journals as the *Yale Review, Story,* the *Southern Review,* the *Chicago Tribune,* the *Antioch Review,* and the *Gettysburg Review.* He lives in Mount Pleasant, South Carolina, and teaches at the College of Charleston, as well as the MFA program at Vermont College.